Becoming Experts: Reading Nonfiction

Lucy Calkins, Series Editor

Amanda Hartman, Celena Dangler Larkey, and Lindsay Wilkes

Photography by Peter Cunningham

Illustrations by Marjorie Martinelli

HEINEMANN ◆ PORTSMOUTH, NH

For Jacob. The world is your oyster. Go out, read about it, and live it.—A.H.

For Gabe. Oh, how I love that you question relentlessly! Everything. And every day.—C.D.L.

For Mom and Dad. For the unconditional love that led me down the path that found me here.—L.W.

Heinemann
361 Hanover Street
Portsmouth, NH 03801–3912
www.heinemann.com

Offices and agents throughout the world

© 2015 by Lucy Calkins, Amanda Hartman, Celena Dangler Larkey, and Lindsay Wilkes

The authors and publisher wish to thank those who have generously given permission to reprint borrowed material:

Reprinted with permission from the book *National Geographic Reader: Tigers*, by Laura Marsh. © 2012 National Geographic Society.

From *Amazing Animals: Tigers*, by Valerie Bodden. Creative Paperback, 2009. © Creative Education is an imprint of The Creative Company, Mankato, MN.

From *Knights in Shining Armor*, by Gail Gibbons. Text and illustrations copyright © 1995 by Gail Gibbons. Used by permission of Little Brown Books for Young Readers.

Tornados! by Gail Gibbons. Holiday House, 2010. Copyright © 2009. Used by permission of Holiday House.

From *Amazing Animals: Monkeys*, by Valerie Boddden. Creative Company, 2011. © Creative Education is an imprint of The Creative Company, Mankato, MN.

New York City in the 1800s, by Branca Tani .© 2011 by The Rosen Publishing Group, Inc. and reprinted with permission. Page 2 image Historic Map Works LLC/Getty, page 4 Brooklyn Bridge image HIP/Art Resource, NY, page 6 elevated train image The New York Public Library/Art Resource, page 7 elevated train image Kean Collection/ Getty.

Materials by Kaeden Books and Lee & Low Books, appearing throughout the primary series, are reproduced by generous permission of the publishers. A detailed list of credits is available in the Grade 2 online resources.

Cataloging-in-Publication data is on file with the Library of Congress.

ISBN-13: 978-0-325-07708-6

Series editorial team: Anna Gratz Cockerille, Karen Kawaguchi, Tracy Wells, Felicia O'Brien, Debra Doorack, Jean Lawler, Marielle Palombo, and Sue Paro
Production: Elizabeth Valway, David Stirling, and Abigail Heim
Cover and interior designs: Jenny Jensen Greenleaf
Photography: Peter Cunningham
Illustrations: Marjorie Martinelli
Composition: Publishers' Design and Production Services, Inc.
Manufacturing: Steve Bernier

Printed in the United States of America on acid-free paper
19 18 17 16 15   PAH   2 3 4 5

Acknowledgments

ONLY A FEW NAMES grace the cover of this book but there are dozens of people and schools that made this book come to life.

This book, or any book in this series, could not *be* without Lucy Calkins. Thank you, for writing long hours with us and for providing the ideas that help to bring more students and teachers into this reading world. Thank you for finding the voice of this book and coaxing our voices at the same time. Your vision, your words, and your example of teaching excellence are ever inspiring and much appreciated. We have learned much about teaching by writing with you.

You can tell a lot about a person by studying the company she keeps, and let us just say, we keep only the *most excellent* of company. Every day the extraordinary community at the Teachers College Reading and Writing Project (TCRWP) seeks to outgrow its best thinking, its best practice, and makes us our best selves. In particular, we thank the leaders—Laurie Pessah, Kathleen Tolan, Mary Ehrenworth (as well as Lucy). We also want to thank Audra Robb, Director of Performance Assessment, and Cheryl Tyler, who leads Reading Rescue. Thank you for your leadership and vision. We value each of you so very much. The primary staff developers at the Project are the most collegial, supportive group of people you could find anywhere. We love the late night phone calls, the text messages with perfectly timed support, the sharing of talents, wisdom, and work. We especially love the straight-up, no-holds-barred feedback. You each added to this book and this series.

Marjorie Martinelli, how we appreciate your talent for making charts that engage, delight, and teach readers to do their very best work! Every book in this series has had the gift of "elves," as we call them—brilliant people who come into the manuscript when authors are away and help move things along, adding a small-group session here, some coaching text there, streamlining a minilesson, adding a share. This book received help from Beth Moore, Nalijah Taylor, Annemarie Johnson, and especially Julia Mooney and Liz Dunford Franco, who have been a constant source of writerly help and of support all along the way. Thank you all for your contributions.

A special thanks to our editors, Sue Paro and Katie Clements, for reading so thoughtfully through our writing and revisions. We are in awe of your dedication and ability to make our ideas and teaching dance down the page with just the right words.

Abby Heim is a constant source of organization and support. We are grateful for her intelligence and humor and for her patience throughout this process. Trust us, we know how exhausting we can be, and Abby's steady pace and calm collectedness is unparalleled. Thank you for every single thing. In a perfect world, every book would be touched by Abby's thoughtful hands and mindful eye. Abby is able to work her wonders because she has the support of so many—Amanda Bondi, Elizabeth Valway, David Stirling, Jenny Jensen Greenleaf, Stephanie Levy, . . . and the list goes on. Those of us at the Project get great pleasure in knowing that when we pass our work along to you, there is a team that works with the same spirit on the second half of the process. We know that you, also, are burning the midnight oil, staying on (and on) to perfect that last detail. Thank you.

While the class described in this unit is a composite class, with children and partnerships gleaned from classrooms in very different contexts and put together here, there are specific teachers and students who piloted this work. We wrote the sessions, but you breathed life into each. The sessions you piloted, the photos and clips of students' thinking, and copies of their work helped shape our vision. Thanks to Katie Linder and Ruth Krause at Poplar Creek and Madison Elementary Schools. Thanks, too, to the principals, teachers, and second-grade teachers at PS 503BK in Brooklyn, PS 89Q, and to United World College South East Asia Dover Campus in Singapore for allowing us to pilot workshop sessions, shared reading, and read-aloud work inside your various classrooms.

—Celena, Lindsay, and Amanda

Contents

BEND III   Reading Across a Topic

Read-Aloud and Shared Reading

An Orientation to the Unit

ALL SYSTEMS ARE GO. Your second-grade reading workshop is off and running. The kids are matched to books, and hopefully many of them are reading up a storm. If your kids are reading with stamina and engagement and if they are happy when it is time to read, celebrate. Your year is off to a good start.

The good news is that for students who are flourishing as readers, this unit will offer them an important new challenge, and for those who may not yet have self-identified as readers, who are not yet sure that reading is their cup of tea, this upcoming unit offers a new way to connect with reading. It may just be that some of these kids will find reading suits them better when they're studying charts, text boxes, and cross-sectional views, and learning about dinosaurs and the Milky Way, race cars and inertia.

So, as this unit begins, you will tell your students that for a time, they'll shift from reading fiction to reading nonfiction. For a time, they'll need to say goodbye to Ivy and Bean and to Captain Underpants.

But, it is time to say hello to nonfiction, and that's a big deal. There is research that suggests that first-grade students read nonfiction for only 3.6 minutes a day. Chances are good that most second-graders don't get much more access to nonfiction than that. So this unit puts you on the cutting edge of primary language arts instruction.

You'll definitely want to use this unit as an opportunity not only to teach skills but also to support your students in developing broader and richer understandings of reading. Think of how much of the reading you do in your life is nonfiction: restaurant reviews, websites, magazines, biographies, high-interest nonfiction books, teaching guides, maps, and travel books. You'll be inviting your children into all of that. Meanwhile, think of the topics they have yet to explore. For most of your students, books about other nations or what happens underground or volcanoes or Congress will all open whole new horizons. By teaching kids to read nonfiction, you teach them to explore and to construct for themselves knowledge of the world. It's a big world out there, and it's just waiting for your students to read it!

To tackle the wide range of nonfiction, you'll set your readers off to read lots of different books on different topics, both familiar and unfamiliar. You'll challenge readers to be the kind of humans who live wide-awake lives, setting themselves up to learn more about topics that are in their schema, as well as set themselves up to become learners of brand-new knowledge. You might say, "Just a few weeks ago I couldn't imagine myself as a gold prospector, but I found this book about the California Gold Rush and I'll tell you, I know more about the Wild West and the quest for new riches than I ever thought possible." With those words, your readers will be off and running.

In the first bend in the road, you will share with your second-graders that to grow knowledge, nonfiction readers must study, notice details, and question texts as they read and put pages of text together. You'll teach readers not only how to approach and navigate through nonfiction texts with questions and ideas in mind but also how to read nonfiction with a voice that matches the content. The work readers do in Bend I transitions to a focus on word solving and vocabulary development as you shift to the second bend in the road, which develops students' vocabulary usage and understanding. Students are introduced to various word-solving and vocabulary-building strategies that teach them how to flexibly and efficiently solve unknown words and use those words as they learn about their topics. From Bend II, you'll move to the third bend in the road, and with that shift, students will begin to read from text sets, choosing a topic to read about, and then connecting, comparing, and contrasting information inside and across texts. You'll prepare your readers to be the kind of readers who read with big questions in mind and carry knowledge from one text to another so that they can add on, confirm, and grow knowledge about their topics.

The bends work together to teach readers to grow knowledge with learning and questioning. We can't wait to share this unit with you. We hope you love it as much as we do.

THE INTERSECTION OF READING DEVELOPMENT AND THIS UNIT

The times, they are a-changin'. Bob Dylan sang those words a long time ago, but they still hold true today. But it is not just the times that are a-changin': the books are a-changin' as well. And the skills needed to navigate those books and the readers choosing those books are a-changin'—all at rapid speed. Buckle up.

Those same readers who started the year on coltish legs are now making their way to more complex texts full of complex topics, vocabulary, and structures. As you shift to this second unit of study, you'll expect most of your readers to be reading levels J/K independently and to be ready to move to up a notch. The jump to levels K and L is a dramatic one. Here's why: There is a noted increase in complexity of text content requiring higher-level comprehension. The texts contain longer parts (chapters, sections, and paragraphs), and they require more accumulation of information across the entire book. And it is not just that the books and the sections of the books are longer; the sentences are longer, too, and they contain complex language structures. Meanwhile the number of multisyllabic words increases dramatically, requiring readers to read across whole words and break them into syllables in order to use the parts they know to figure out these difficult words. This makes heavy demands on students' skills and requires them to reach for new strategies.

There is no one thing that readers need to do to read fluently, but more a myriad of skills. The challenge is that they need to use those skills with automaticity and flexibility, so they can free enough mind space to think about the concepts and ideas that are being introduced. The books are often teaching content that is outside of the known for kids, topics such as space, history, different cultures, and scientific processes.

The content-specific and technical words used to write about these sophisticated topics often tax kids' word-solving skills. As readers move into higher levels, the texts become more vocabulary-rich. While children may be able to decode a word, they won't necessarily understand the word once it has been pronounced.

As second-graders continue to read texts that are longer, they need to learn to navigate text structures that are more complicated and varied for nonfiction than for fiction texts at these levels. As fiction readers, your children have become accustomed to leaning on the structure of stories and on their knowledge of the character to anticipate the plot's typical trajectory. Now that readers are reading nonfiction, they'll learn that nonfiction readers work hard to put key details together to determine the subject's main topic so they can learn what the pages or parts of a book are striving to teach. They'll find, however, that different texts work in different ways. Your students will learn that to do their best learning from the texts, they should use the structure of the texts to support them in organizing what they learn.

As children become more proficient, they will still encounter difficulty with tricky words and make miscues. The books your children are reading will be far more challenging than those they used to read, and they'll definitely encounter unfamiliar vocabulary words that will pose challenges for them. They need to be ready to use context to help them figure out what a word is apt to mean. To engage in that sort of figuring-out work, readers need to monitor for sense and to stop at the point of error, rather than just skipping past or mumbling over the tricky words. Teaching readers to word solve using context takes on new meaning, because readers increasingly need to not just "read around" the word, but rather think about the whole page in order to figure out meaning. As readers do this work, one of the challenges will be for them to shift into the micro-level work with a challenging word, while not dropping their grip on the larger content that is being taught in the book.

Just as you'll find children who read above benchmark, you'll also have readers still striving to get to benchmark. Their nonfiction texts will work in different ways: they'll be simpler, with less vocabulary and fewer text features. While it's true that the texts these readers read independently work differently, the word-solving work that readers at levels G, H, and I need to do is tackling trouble at the point of error.

We've talked about the reading development work that this unit will be supporting—some of which can occur as children read nonfiction, but is actually independent of genre—but an important part of the job of learning to read nonfiction well involves learning to *learn*. Think about this for yourself. Say you want to learn more about a topic—say, Twitter. Or the Austro-Hungarian Empire. You've got so many questions, and you know you lack foundational knowledge. So what do you do? If you feel as if you want to undertake a course of study on a topic, do you tend to go to a friend and say, "Can you give me a little course on—?" Or are you just as apt to sit down with some texts and make your way among them, letting those texts take you step by step along in a course of study on whatever your topic might be? We ask this, because part of the job of this unit is that you are teaching your kids that they can actually learn about a topic in the world without needing a teacher. Books can be their teacher.

It is a big deal to teach readers that they can read to take in new knowledge. They need to know that part of what they will do in their minds as they read is to compare new knowledge to known knowledge, and to compare and contrast information they learn from one text to another and maybe to yet another. You'll also want to teach them that to learn from texts, it helps to actually read a bunch of the text—a chunk of it—all at a time, in a swoop, and only afterward pause and think, "What did I just learn?" At those pauses to accumulate, it helps to ask, "Was what I just learned the same as what I already knew? Did it add on? Change things?"

Fiction at these levels is often tidily organized into chapters or parts, helping readers put entire texts together by connecting the parts. Nonfiction at these levels sometimes does this work, but sometimes it does not.

Second-graders, because they can now read and write with greater fluency, view successful reading as *fast*. They're zooming to accumulate the most pages, and the most books—the faster the better, in a second-grader's mind. You'll teach into the need for fluency development, but you won't push for faster reading; instead, you'll coach for phrasing and intonation. As readers take on more complex sentences, it is important, yes, that they note and read the punctuation inside and at the end of sentences, pausing and changing voice to match meaning of the texts. But it will be the reader's thinking, the reader's understanding of the text, that actually makes the text sound intelligent. Readers need a felt sense for what it means to understand nonfiction. Of course, the fluency that matters the most will be the fluency of readers' in-the-head reading, because at this level, students read texts silently unless there is some reason to do otherwise.

Partnerships will become increasingly powerful this year. Research tells us that every reader, every day, needs opportunities to talk about texts. In this unit, you'll leverage those social relationships during partner time and tightly forge links to power your teaching. Partnerships will continue to be of utmost importance. The partnerships you establish during this unit of study will support your readers as they compare and contrast information across texts.

Second-graders want to be heard. What they have to say and what they've learned matters. They need to know others see them as "big kids." They want the world to acknowledge them as experts on their stuff—they know all about Minecraft, soccer, and puppies, and they need opportunities to show off what they know. The nonfiction work in this unit allows for those opportunities.

OVERVIEW

The unit ahead is divided into three bends. Bend I focuses students' attention on growing knowledge as they pay attention to details, put parts of text together, and question texts. Bend II works to tackle both the tricky word work and vocabulary development students need to navigate nonfiction reading. Bend III sets readers up to grow knowledge across texts as they read topic sets of texts, comparing, contrasting, and connecting information across texts and text sets and doing the vocabulary work that accompanies nonfiction reading.

Bend I: Thinking Hard and Growing Knowledge

The first bend sets the readers up for noticing, learning from, and questioning texts, both traditional and nontraditional. To launch the unit, you'll gather items—globes, diagrams, a model sarcophagus, maps of your city or subway system, a plastic human eyeball model, whatever you can get your hands on—for students to study closely, notice details in, and learn from as they grow knowledge. You'll lean in and say, "Readers, today starts a brand-new unit of study in our reading workshop. To get started, instead of reading a book, will you 'read' our meeting area, our environment, and other *things*. Read whatever you see in the meeting area that tells about our upcoming unit and *think* really hard in order to put together for yourself—in your own brain—a sense of what this unit will be about. Go!" This sets the course for all that lies ahead in the bend as you teach readers that nonfiction texts are chock-full of amazing details and information that they'll read to learn, to grow, and to become experts on various topics of their choice.

You'll teach children that nonfiction readers read texts, intent on learning about a topic. Researchers emphasize that as the nonfiction reader proceeds through a text—say, an article about tadpoles becoming frogs—the reader continually adds to a mental model of the topic. You won't talk to kids about "building a mental model," but you will teach youngsters to read in that sort of way: reading words on the page and thinking, "How does what I just learned fit with my growing knowledge of the topic?" This sort of reading requires a rhythm of read/think/read. The unit begins with dramatizing the ratio between reading and thinking when you have students read texts that have only a few words but provoke a lot of thinking. In the first two sessions, your readers will be reading charts, diagrams, directions, and models, and your teaching will focus on the great amount of thinking you hope accompanies that small amount of reading.

Once your youngsters begin to read nonfiction books, you'll continue to highlight the thinking they need to do. They'll do the big work of questioning what the book will teach them, and they'll prepare themselves to read wide-awake, on the lookout for new and unknown information and ideas. You'll teach readers to think, "What is this text about?" to set themselves up to understand the structure of their nonfiction texts and to gather knowledge in efficient and effective ways. You'll teach them to ask that question before they even start to read, after they read a little, and again after they read more, and they will notice that the answer will change (usually becoming more specific): "It's about birds . . . birds' beaks . . . different kinds of birds' beaks."

Also, you'll help readers know that when they alternate between reading and thinking, they will find it beneficial to think not only "What does the book say?" but also "What's important about this?" and "What do I think about this?" Students will use text features, such as headings, to help them figure out what a part of the text is mostly about, identifying the main topic and key details.

As the bend winds down, you'll teach readers about the gift of learning. You'll introduce your readers to the "book fairy," calling them quickly to the rug to show a fancily wrapped gift and telling them, "You are not going to believe this, but last night, I think a *book fairy* must have come to our classroom. Because look what was here on my chair when I arrived this morning!" You'll reveal a beautifully wrapped gift, with an extra-fancy profusion of bows. In this way, you'll teach nonfiction readers how to be the sort of readers who read for surprises, gifts of knowledge. You'll say, "Today, I want to teach you that one of the best things about books is that even after you take a sneak peek and you anticipate what the book will probably teach you, there will be surprises. Usually, the places where books surprise you are the places where they teach you the most, so be glad for the surprises."

Bend II: Learning the Lingo of a Topic

The next bend focuses on the hard and flexible work readers need to do as they solve tricky words, concepts, and domain-specific vocabulary inside their nonfiction reading books. You will remind kids that reading nonfiction is not easy and that they need to bring all their perseverance to this job. You'll highlight how nonfiction readers aquire and use new vocabulary to learn about and understand topics. To start the bend you'll say, "Readers think, 'What keywords do I expect to run into?' and they generate a little list. Later, when readers encounter one of those words in the book, they don't get as stuck. Instead, they think, 'I *knew* that word would be here!'" Any new topic brings new language. You'll show readers how to prepare to take in that new language and vocabulary by being on the lookout for those words and phrases and by taking time to consider what words readers might meet within the book.

Your students will learn not to shy away from studying and learning from the rich features that nonfiction texts include to teach readers about topics. Too often, children collect nonfiction features like Pokémon cards. They may know what a feature is called and where to find it, but you'll teach them to take the time to develop an understanding of how it works to teach readers important and varied information about a topic. They'll learn to use text boxes, boldfaced words, and features such as a glossary and an index to read closely, talk about topics, and grow vocabulary. You'll teach them to read features not only to learn from but also to check their understanding. You'll say, "Readers, just like you can use a glossary to find and understand keywords, you can use it to check your understanding. Give yourself a pop quiz with the glossary!" and kids will become engaged in learning with features of texts. Fun!

When readers do encounter tricky vocabulary, they need to draw upon a repertoire of strategies, like keys that unlock doors. You'll say, "Today I want to teach you that when readers are stuck on a keyword, they know to play around with the word, like you might play around with a key in the lock—trying it first one way and then another, and sometimes—presto!—the lock opens." You and your students will work together across and around words to unlock key vocabulary in and make meaning from text.

You'll teach children how to be flexible and fluid in their use of word-solving strategies, trying one strategy after another to not just *say* what's on the page but to really understand what the word means or how the word works.

You'll model how to use phonics and word-solving strategies to get as close as possible to how a word sounds and then how to use the whole page, the part of the book, and maybe the topic to really comprehend what the word or concept *means* in the text. You'll also teach readers the importance of thinking and sharing their learning with others, using the vocabulary that goes along with their topics, as they determine main topics and key details in texts. Your partnerships will join into groups of four, creating "rug clubs," places to talk the talk and walk the walk of a topic. You'll lead students in using their books and keywords to teach a couple of the most important things they have learned. You'll say, "Remember, listeners, don't just take in information; ask questions like or 'What do you mean? Can you say more about that?'" as the readers read, talk, and grow knowledge together.

Bend III: Across a Topic

At the start of Bend III, you'll start by standing in the midst of your readers, exclaiming, "Readers, before you come to the meeting area, look up here! The book fairy has done it *again*!" You'll hold your discovery high, for all to see, and show another lavishly wrapped mystery book, bound together with your well-worn copy of *Tigers* by Laura Marsh. You'll show students how books are put together to make text sets, and you'll set students up to topic shop—to think about a topic and to *preview* a topic by thinking how the books will teach and what information is likely to be inside each text.

You'll show them how to think about a topic as they take sneak peeks and compare parts of texts. Your students will read and find parts that go together and they'll look at how the texts are structured to figure out how the books go together or to decide in which order they should read their books to make the most meaning.

You'll teach readers the big work of comparing and contrasting information inside texts, as well as how to compare and contrast information across different texts. You'll teach them how to notice when information is new or different and how to mark those spots. You'll also teach the hard task of getting rid of misunderstood and inaccurate information and replacing it with correct information. This is no easy feat. The end of the bend is celebratory in nature. Hard work deserves recognition! You'll notice we have a couple of

sessions designed both to prepare for the celebration and to savor the work of nonfiction reading as part of the final celebration.

The unit celebration takes your nonfiction readers truly into the realm of experts on a topic by inviting the class to turn into museum tour guides and practice leading reading exhibitions for classroom visitors. You'll present a short clip of a real museum curator talking about how to best prepare to teach others, and you'll set the readers up to prepare for their own exhibits. A fancy red ribbon, some clip-on tour guide buttons, oversize scissors (if you can find them), and maybe even a bit of ceremonial music will enhance the unveiling of your reading museum. Your students will meet their visitors at the door (perhaps the big kids from the fifth-grade wing of the school, parents or guardians, a stray grandma or grandpa here and there), who will come in to listen to your experts teach their topics of expertise.

ASSESSMENT

Conduct and gather data from formal and informal running records.

First, you will want to continue to use your running records to help you think about reading process and how your students are using and integrating the sources of information as they read. At this point in the year (late fall/early winter), you should expect your readers to be approaching levels J/K/L in order to achieve the end-of-year benchmark. You will probably need to take running records to determine how your kids are approaching grade-level text complexity. Analyzing (formal or informal) running records will give insight into the strategies your students rely on for decoding, fluency, and comprehension, and it will help you keep track of their progress up the gradient of book difficulty. Doing a miscue analysis to determine how children are integrating sources of information will also help you make decisions about what print work to teach each of your readers next. If you find that when reading fiction, a student stops on a hard word and uses only phonics to say it, it is likely that she does the same in nonfiction books. You'll want to help such students set a goal to cross-check what they say and ask themselves, "Does that make sense? Do I know a word that sounds similar that would match the information in the book?" This is an important goal in reading, regardless of the genre.

Conduct further assessments to design instructional goals for word study and reading.

Second, you will continue to use a spelling inventory to determine what types of phonics features to work on in word study, writing, and reading. Also, you will want to be sure that your high-frequency word list is up-to-date and that you know where students are. You can expect that most second-graders will have mastered the words on the TCRWP High-Frequency Word Assessment by midyear.

Assess a few comprehension skills students need to develop in reading nonfiction books.

Listen to students talk about books during read-aloud, conferences, and partner talk times. Pay special attention to the work taught in this unit: main ideas, questions, vocabulary, and accumulating information across texts. During read-aloud you may want to look at a few particular comprehension skills in nonfiction reading, such as raising and answering questions about key details in the text, learning new words while reading, identifying the main topic, or comparing and contrasting information across texts.

During a regular read-aloud experience, you might choose a few parts where you will ask kids to do some quick stop-and-sketch and jot assessments. For example, you may ask students to stop and jot on Post-its or on a sheet of paper to respond to the text. You might read a section and ask students to jot a heading that describes what that section is mostly about, or you may ask students to jot questions about the text. After a reading several sections, you might ask students to jot what they think the main topic of the book may be. To assess comparing and contrasting, you might say, "Hmm, these two things seem very similar, but they have some important differences. Right now, stop and jot one thing that is similar about these two things. Now jot one important difference."

Asking kids to stop and sketch or jot quick responses is one way to collect some information about reading comprehension. In some instances you might want to interview students further about what they are jotting or sketching, much like kindergarten teachers do on a writing assessment. This gives you a little window to see what students' understanding is of a particular skill that you can then work on and grow in this unit of study.

At the end of the unit, you could select different texts to read aloud and assess students' responses to them. By placing student responses from this summative assessment alongside the Post-its from the beginning of the unit, you will be able to determine how students have grown as a result of your teaching. This information will also inform the new goals you set for yourself as you plan your teaching in the content areas and a spring information unit of study. You may want to turn to the *Reading Pathways* book for grades 3–5 to think more about the progression of comprehension skills.

Use assessment data to tailor your plans for instruction.

You can refer to *If . . . Then . . . Curriculum: Assessment-Based Instruction, Grades K–2* as a resource. The alternate unit "Growing Expertise in Little Books: Nonfiction Reading" can serve as a supplement to this unit if your assessments reveal that you have a group of readers at levels C–G. This unit can guide your small-group work with students reading at those levels.

You can also look to the unit titled "Reading Nonfiction Cover to Cover: Nonfiction Book Clubs," also in *If . . . Then . . . Curriculum, Grades K–2*, to extend the work of this unit, especially if your students are reading on or even above the benchmark. This unit will provide more practice reading across texts—this time with a new spin—reading about and talking about nonfiction topics in clubs. You might select particular bends and insert them into this unit as extensions—keeping in mind that a unit ideally lasts approximately six weeks. If a unit lasts too long, students will become disengaged and your teaching won't be effective. Alternatively (probably preferably), you might decide to teach the nonfiction book clubs unit later in the year as a return to nonfiction reading, this time in the form of clubs.

You may decide that your next unit will be "Studying Characters and Their Stories," available in the online resources for *If . . . Then . . . Curriculum, Grades K–2*, a unit designed for transitional readers at levels H–L. This unit will build on the work of the first-grade unit *Meeting Characters and Learning Lessons: A Study of Story Elements* and will provide support your students may need for reading early chapter books, before diving into *Series Books Clubs* later in the year, in Unit 4. Teaching "Studying Characters and Their Stories" in the first half of your school year will also provide a welcome balance of fiction and nonfiction across your year.

GETTING READY

Gather diagrams, maps, rules for games, globes, and so on for students to read for a day or two before transitioning them to shop for more traditional leveled nonfiction texts.

If you read the start of this unit, you'll see that you'll be teaching your students to read fewer words but to think more—and that you'll do this by channeling them to read maps, diagrams, charts, labeled models, directions, and so forth. You might set forth a globe, a model of the human heart, a solar system diagram: go for nonfiction "texts" that are as engaging and varied as possible and that can help you make the point that readers of nonfiction read and then think, instead of whipping along through words, sentences, and pages. Think about the world of nonfiction reading, and include items that will enrich your students' understanding of all that nonfiction entails. The goal will be for kids to read slowly and thoughtfully, noticing details, and putting parts together to ask questions and grow understandings. For just this first day, we suggest you steer clear of books that students are accustomed to leafing through.

It won't be long at all before you transition your children to shop for just-right nonfiction texts, so you will also want to take stock of your nonfiction library. Your children will need to refill their bins with nonfiction texts every week, and they'll need from eight to ten nonfiction texts at a time.

We hope you can round up enough nonfiction books so that when you say, at the end of each day's minilesson, "Off you go," and kids head to their reading spots, they'll have baggies full of nonfiction books that they can read with comprehension. This unit was written in hopes that you have a well-provisioned nonfiction library, so that students can "shop" for nonfiction books, filling their baggies with a small collection of books that they read and sometimes reread before returning them and fetching another baggie full. In order to make the unit as practical as possible, we planned it so that in the first two bends, the books that a reader puts into his or her baggie do not necessarily have to be topic-based—that is, a child may have one book on bears, one on robots, and so on. It would be better, of course, if those books were always rubber-banded in with other books on similar levels and topics.

Just a note: When children read on a topic of special expertise (as when a baseball enthusiast reads a baseball book), or when you are able to provide readers with support so they can work with books a notch higher, children can read books at their instructional level.

If you don't have enough nonfiction books for your class of children to each keep ten just-right books in their baggie for a week, then you'll need to do some thinking about alternate ways to proceed. Here are some suggestions that have worked for teachers in this situation:

- Encourage children to read fiction as well as nonfiction.

- Suggest that children don't "own" nonfiction books privately, but instead keep books in a bin at the center of a table. Seat kids who are reading from that particular level of text difficulty around the bin. This way, each child has only one book in his or her possession at any time.

- Make a traveling cart of nonfiction books that will move from classroom to classroom. In this scenario, one second grade has reading workshop first period, another schedules reading workshop second period, and so on.

If you encourage children to read fiction as well as nonfiction . . .

Although it is important for children to grow up with a balanced diet, reading a roughly equal division of fiction and nonfiction, the most important thing is that kids engage in an enormous volume of reading and reading those books with comprehension. So right from the start, decide whether you can round up enough nonfiction books for your children to read only nonfiction for the duration of this unit. If channeling them toward nonfiction will mean they need to cycle again and again through the same small set of books or to read books that they can't comprehend, those are not viable options. You might instead divide your reading time into chunks, and save time for fiction as well as nonfiction reading. You might shorten the time spent reading (nonfiction) between the minilesson and the share and then, after each day's share, invite kids to spend ten minutes reading their fiction book. If you make that choice, keep charts from Unit 1 alive to lift the level of that fiction reading. Send those fiction books home, as well as the nonfiction books (or send fiction books home instead of nonfiction, if your supply of nonfiction is especially low).

If you suggest that children don't "own" nonfiction books privately but instead put books in a bin at the center of a table and seat kids who are reading from that particular level of text difficulty around the bin . . .

Another option is for partners to share baggies, so that instead of each reader needing ten just-right nonfiction books each week, every two readers will need that many. If even that is not possible, you can put the nonfiction books at a certain level of text difficulty in a bin at the center of a table and seat children who can read those books around that table. Each child can mark his or her current book with a Post-it so that if a child doesn't complete a book in one reading time, he or she can find it in the pile the next day.

If you make traveling carts of nonfiction books and send these from classroom to classroom . . .

If you have a very small collection of nonfiction books, then try the idea of a rolling cart that carries books from one classroom to another, with class-rooms staggering when reading time occurs.

You'll notice in the third bend that we suggest that you create leveled, topic-based sets that include related nonfiction books (say, one baggie has a small pile of level H/I books on castles plus an Inside Outside castle book) and that children can shop for multiple text sets to grow deeper knowledge about fewer topics by reading across books.

Select and gather books and texts for minilessons and guided reading.

You'll want to gather the texts that you will use for minilesson and small-group work. We suggest using texts that provide engaging information and oppor-tunities for the comprehension work you'll carry across subsequent lessons. You can also use songs from movies like *The Lion King* or *The Jungle Book* to show kids how readers gain information from many kinds of texts. You'll noticed that we've used the read-aloud text *Knights in Shining Armor* by Gail Gibbons, and the shared reading text *Tigers* by Laura Marsh, across the first two bends of the unit. You can also use a couple of different texts, any that you have in your shelves, in these first two bends. Those other texts are entirely optional. For the third bend, it will be important to select a text that connects to a text you used within the first two bends and will support the compare-and-contrast work you'll invite readers to do. We've chosen *Amazing Animals: Tigers* by Valerie Bodden, which differs from the shared reading text *Tigers* in its layout and structure, but offers similar content for readers to use to practice growing knowledge across books.

You will also want to gather texts to use in your guided-reading and shared-reading small groups. Unless children have recently moved into their current level of text difficulty, you'll want to choose a text that is one level above their current just-right book level. For some of your students, that will mean an unfamiliar level K or L book.

Continue to use, create, and distribute reading tools.

Continue to use the bookmarks, reading logs, Post-its, and take-home book baggies to keep up the routines you launched in the first unit. You'll want to keep some charts from the first unit accessible, to continue to reinforce the reading strategies and routines that readers are becoming more proficient in. You'll also want to create some new charts to give readers a tangible reminder of the nonfiction skills and strategies they will learn to use in this unit.

Also to prepare for the new unit, you may decide to have readers study the reading logs they've kept thus far in the year and make plans for what they'll do as the new unit begins. You might ask students to set goals for themselves as they prepare for the unit to come. It may be, too, that as you study your readers' independent reading levels, you'll find that they would benefit from logging their reading lives in a new, more sophisticated way.

Use the read-aloud plan at the back of this book to prepare for one read-aloud across a couple of days, as well as others across the unit.

The books you choose for read-aloud will set your students up to learn from texts. Research shows that children—even children as old as sixteen—benefit from having books read aloud to them. It is no small matter to make time in your schedule to read aloud and engage children in rich conversation around texts.

Generally the texts you read aloud will be at higher levels of text complex-ity than those your children are reading independently. You may, for example, want to choose read-alouds that are in the level M/N range. We chose *Knights in Shining Armor* by Gail Gibbons for the first nonfiction read-aloud.

Select books that include engaging and complex information that will be fun to talk and think about.

Knights in Shining Armor has many elements that make it a great choice for the start of second grade. First, who isn't interested in knighthood? Then, too, the text has a complex text structure. It begins teaching about the earli-est knights and their jobs, and then shifts to a timeline of how a young boy became a knight. Later portions of the book teach readers about types of knights, battles, and weapons. Then the book jumps ahead in time and dis-cusses modern-day knighthood and ends with legends written around knights. The many different sections of the book offer readers many opportunities to think, "What's this part about?" and show readers that books often contain different parts. The book is also rich in vocabulary and information. Children will learn not only about knights and their roles in history but also about medieval times and the European feudal system.

The read-aloud plan at the back of this book will help you support student thinking. During the first read-through of the book, we give you prompts to engage your students in taking a meaningful sneak peek of the book and to support making, confirming, and revising their predictions. Later your students will get support retelling important parts of the text. The read-aloud divides the text into two separate read-throughs, and then, on the third day, you will reread selected parts closely.

Choose other texts you may want to read aloud.

Use the Post-it notes, with the prompts written on them, which you can place directly into your own copy of the book. We imagine that you will then be able to take out these Post-it notes and use them in another read-aloud text that you select. All of the prompts are transferable and intended to be used across texts. Continue to select nonfiction texts to read aloud that are engaging and offer opportunities for children to practice the comprehension work that this unit strives to teach. Select texts that are complex, as you will be there to scaffold their thinking and demonstrate how to read nonfiction texts from cover to cover, while considering all the information the author intended for the reader to learn about the topic.

Use the five-day plan in the back of this book to help you prepare for shared reading.

After the read-aloud template in the back of the book, you will find a five-day plan for shared reading. We've chosen to use *Tigers* by Laura Marsh. This plan is meant to be a template for how you can complement the teaching in this unit across a week. Our hope is that you'll use the template and replicate it often, reteaching the important work of the unit with several other shared reading texts for the remaining weeks.

Select books that will teach the main skills that echo your unit and what your students need as readers.

We selected *Tigers* by Laura Marsh for several reasons. First, this text matches where many of your readers will be in terms of reading level. This text is a level J and will offer a lot of good work for readers to develop the nonfiction skills and strategies that they will utilize across books. This text is also a part of the National Geographic Kids series, which is chock-full of engaging information, gorgeous photographs, and helpful text features.

☙ ONLINE DIGITAL RESOURCES

A variety of resources to accompany this and the other Grade 2 Units of Study for Teaching Reading are available in the Online Resources, including charts and examples of student work shown throughout *Becoming Experts*, as well as links to other electronic resources. Offering daily support for your teaching, these materials will help you provide a structured learning environment that fosters independence and self-direction.

To access and download all the digital resources for the Grade 2 Units of Study for Teaching Reading:

1. Go to **www.heinemann.com** and click the link in the upper right to log in. (If you do not have an account yet, you will need to create one.)

2. **Enter the following registration code** in the box to register your product: RUOS_Gr2

3. Under **My Online Resources**, click the link for the **Grade 2 Reading Units of Study**.

4. The digital resources are available in the upper right; click a file name to download. (For any compressed ("ZIP") files, double-click the downloaded file to extract individual files to your hard drive.)

(You may keep copies of these resources on up to six of your own computers or devices. By downloading the files you acknowledge that they are for your individual or classroom use and that neither the resources nor the product code will be distributed or shared.)

Nonfiction Readers
Notice and Learn

IN THIS SESSION, you'll teach children that nonfiction readers pay attention to the details, the bits and pieces, putting all this together to *really* understand and grow knowledge about a topic.

GETTING READY

✓ Reorganize your library to support nonfiction reading (see Getting Ready in An Orientation to the Unit). Have on hand a few high-interest nonfiction books that you can use to preview the enticing content of the upcoming unit (see Connection).

✓ Display the new anchor chart, "Readers Grow Knowledge," with the strategies "Pay attention to details." and "Put the parts of the text together in your mind." in place (see Connection, Teaching, and Link).

✓ Choose a read-aloud text that is above the current benchmark. We use *Knights in Shining Armor*, by Gail Gibbons. If you choose another text, use one that provides engaging information and opportunities for comprehension work. You can use a document camera to project the text during demonstrations, if one is available (see Teaching).

✓ Arrange tables with bins of a few nonfiction texts that tend to be light in words but heavy in drawings, labels, and meaning (such as maps of your town or school, diagrams, or picture books that provide a lot to study in a few pages). In each bin, you may also include fascinating objects (not texts, per se) that can be "read"—a plastic model of the ear/body/stomach, the inner workings of a machine, or a puzzling natural object (see Link).

✓ Select a few texts from the bins for students to study (see Active Engagement and Link).

✓ Post-Its® for students to mark important things they notice so that they can share them later (see Conferring and Small-Group Work).

✓ Assign partners. You may choose to continue partnerships from the previous unit or to rearrange partnerships (see Share).

✓ Ask students to bring a text that they studied to the meeting area (see Share).

✓ Use a few empty cereal boxes to demonstrate that nonfiction readers see and read texts everywhere (see Share).

MINILESSON

CONNECTION

Ask kids to read the materials in the meeting area to grow knowledge about the unit, using this as a metaphor for how nonfiction readers read to construct knowledge.

"Readers, today starts a brand new unit of study in our reading workshop. To get started, instead of reading a book, will you 'read' our meeting area, our environment, and other *things*. Read whatever you see in the meeting area that tells about our upcoming unit and *think* really hard to put together for yourself—in your own brain—a sense of what that unit will be about. Do this alone. No talking; zip your lips. Go!"

As kids started looking around the room, I said to a few (in a stage whisper so others heard), "Will you read the room like this?" and I darted my eyes quickly around the meeting area. "No way! Really study the details."

After a minute, I called, "Turn and talk! What will our unit be about?"

The question was easy, and the room exploded with talk. After a bit, I voiced over, "What *specifically* do you think you'll be taught?" and I listened to what kids expected a unit on nonfiction would entail.

Point out that the reading work kids just did is actually what nonfiction readers do whenever they put together the details of what they see to grow knowledge.

"Eyes up," I said. "You are right that we're starting a unit on nonfiction. Just now—when you read all the details of our meeting area to put together *knowledge* of our next unit, you were doing what nonfiction readers do. Nonfiction readers read nonfiction to grow *knowledge* about the world."

 Name the teaching point.

"Today I want to teach you that readers of nonfiction books do an extra-brainy, intense kind of thinking. Readers pay attention to details and think, 'How can I put together what I'm seeing to grow *knowledge* of this topic?'"

I revealed the new anchor chart and added two Post-it points to it.

ANCHOR CHART

Nonfiction Readers Grow Knowledge
- Pay attention to details.
- Put the parts of the text together in your mind.

TEACHING

Explain that readers study the details of the text, asking, "How can I put this together to grow knowledge of the topic?" Demonstrate by reading a giant diagram.

"Can I give you a few hints about how to do this brainy work of reading to grow knowledge?" I asked. After receiving some nods, I began. "It helps to pay attention to details, to see specifics. It can help to think to yourself, 'I notice . . . ,' but you don't just grab on to *one* detail that you notice. You look at all the parts of the page, of the text, and you try to put what you are learning together in your mind.

"Watch and listen closely to make sure I'm doing that sort of brainy reading, and if I'm not, let me know."

I glanced at the picture of an enlarged chart of a castle from Gail Gibbons's book, *Knights in Shining Armor*, that was placed under the document camera, and with a sweep of the hand, said, "It's a castle," then brushed the picture to the side. The kids protested immediately.

You are asking kids to read the bins and charts around the meeting area to construct knowledge of the upcoming unit, just as you will soon ask them to read other texts—a labeled illustration, eventually a penny—to construct knowledge. You are deliberately asking them to read a limited number of words and to do a maximum amount of thinking, and you are asking them to read to learn. Include artifacts that your English language learners will be able to identify so that everyone can successfully participate in the activity.

Notice that you'll deliberately mess up, reading the nonfiction text in a cursory, off-handed fashion and then self-correct, this time reading thoughtfully. The repetition of the phrase, "I notice . . ." provides a concrete language children can use to do similar thinking work with other texts.

Correcting myself, I said, "Oh, you're right. That wasn't very brainy work. I wasn't paying much attention to all the details. Let me try again. I know it helps to pay attention to details, to see specifics." I traced my finger across the details of the illustration, leaning in to study the image with care. "*I notice* that there is water all around the outside edge. *I notice* that there are also tall towers all around with windows in the towers. There are towers at each corner and towers in the middle of the walls.

"Let me put these details together in my mind to grow knowledge about the topic. Hmm . . . , the water around the castle, the towers. The big thing I'm learning is that castles are built to protect people."

Debrief by naming what you have demonstrated that you hope kids do whenever they read nonfiction texts—or the world.

"Readers, the way I read this diagram of a castle is the way that nonfiction readers read *anything*. I could have just glanced at it like this," and I shot a passing glance at the diagram. "Instead, I looked closely at the details and thought about them; I put what I saw together, trying to make knowledge about castles."

ACTIVE ENGAGEMENT

Channel kids in each quadrant of the meeting area to work together to notice details and put together knowledge about texts you distribute to that group.

"Your turn! You game to try this? I'm going to put something that you can read at the center of each quadrant of our meeting area." I showed what I meant by *quadrant*, gesturing toward the four corners of the carpet. I handed one quadrant a map of the city to study, while another got a model of the human eyeball, and the final two quadrants received other items to read. "Will you guys do that brainy sort of thinking where you study this—stuff?"

"Go!"

As the children worked, I circled among the groups, voicing over tips and reminders such as these:

◆ Look at all the details, the parts.

◆ Say what you notice.

◆ Put together what you see to make knowledge about the topic.

This is a nice chance for some quick assessment. You may want to grab your clipboard and listen in as students turn and share their thinking with partners. Gauge their engagement with the unit. How are they talking about the unit ahead? Student talk at the launch of a unit can offer insight into how you will want to plan your early days in the unit.

LINK

Remind kids of your point and send them off to read diagrams, maps, charts, a globe, models—putting together knowledge as they read.

"Readers, can I call you back? Today you're going to continue to have a chance to read and do this brainy work. You'll read nonfiction today. It might not be the sort of nonfiction you were expecting! Keep in mind the questions, 'What do I notice?' and 'How can I put together what I'm seeing to learn about this topic?'" I gestured to the new anchor chart as a reminder of what nonfiction readers do to grow knowledge.

ANCHOR CHART

Nonfiction Readers Grow Knowledge

- Pay attention to details.
- Put the parts of the text together in your mind.

Note that you are sending kids off to read from a bin of texts—not books—but, instead, diagrams, photographs, maps, and so on, and you are expecting them to work alone, quietly, until it is time for partnership reading.

You'll have distributed charts, diagrams, directions—any nonfiction but books.

FIG. 1–1 Gather a mixture of objects and texts for students to study closely.

FIG. 1–2 Students studying objects and texts closely as nonfiction readers

Channeling Readers to Think Deeply

WHEREAS USUALLY YOU'LL SEND KIDS OFF, book baggie in hand, to read a stack of books that are at their levels, today you will send kids off to read and think about a different sort of collection of texts: a model of the human eye, a map of your city, a chart of animal families, a page of Lego directions. The rigor of kids' work today will not come from the actual amount of print they'll digest (because for today, it will be a negligible amount), but from the thinking you hope they do as they work to grow knowledge. Of course, the limited volume of print is deliberate.

You are essentially hoping to decrease the amount of time spent deciphering words to increase the amount of thinking. This means that you won't need to expend much energy channeling children to pay attention to the "text" they're given. For at least a few minutes, that attention should be ensured. But what you *will* need to do is to channel them to construct knowledge from studying what you put in their hands. Because children won't be reading through books that hold them to the task just by the sequence of pages, you will probably find that they need some way to help them sustain attention. You might, therefore, be prepared to coach children to use Post-its to mark important things they notice so that later they can share these. You will need to decide if you want them jotting on those Post-its or not.

As kids read a model of the human eye or a map of the city, your job will be to help them read attentively and to construct knowledge from what they see. Channeling them to do this is no small task, when they're apt to read a model or diagram like this: "Ew! Disgusting." "Hey, that comes out!" "Let me snap it in." "This part looks like a boat."

If you ask questions such as "What do you notice?" and "What does that make you wonder?" you can channel kids toward a maximum amount of thinking. Your hope is that their thinking is less of the "Gross!" type and more "It is kinda like the eye has layers. Maybe that's because . . ."

Be sure to support your English language learners' participation in this activity. Regardless of their level of language proficiency, this opportunity to use language will strengthen their communication skills. Research suggests that you may need to modify your questions so that even a one-word answer can be acceptable, and that is a wise thing to do if that's what it takes for students in the early stages of language acquisition to participate.

MID-WORKSHOP TEACHING
Readers Have a Choice—To Glance or to *Reread*

"Readers, eyes on me," I said, standing in the middle of the room, and I waited for their focus. "I want to remind you that you have a choice. You can read a book or a chart or anything, really, like this," and I gave a fleeting glance at a globe that one group had been reading. "But you can also read that same object like this. Watch me." I studied the globe, and said, "*I notice* the globe has many colors, but there is more blue than any other color. *I notice* some parts of the globe don't even have a label or a name. *The knowledge I'm growing about this is* that there's a lot of ocean in the world.

"The really important thing is for you to know you have a choice. You can read anything like this," and I gave another fleeting glance, "or you can read like this," and I read carefully, studiously. "Nonfiction readers grow a lot of knowledge from studying things really thoughtfully."

Noticing Details to Grow Knowledge
It Takes Two to Read!

Channel children to identify Partner 1 and 2 and then to read a text to each other and talk about what the reader noticed. Encourage the listening partner to embellish on those observations.

"Readers, a famous researcher once said, 'It takes two to read a book.' Of course, it's not just when reading books but also when reading a chart or a model of the eye or a recipe that reading with another person helps. When two people read, you notice more and you think more. So right now, get with your partner. Decide who will be Partner 1 and who will be Partner 2 for this unit."

They did this. "Partner 1, will you show Partner 2 one important part of the text you read today? Read that thing to your partner, and say, '*I noticed* . . .' and then say, "*And* I also noticed . . . , and I *also* noticed . . .'

"Partner 2, when your partner reads something to you and says, '*I notice* . . . ,' read that text yourself as well, and think about it. *Really* think. What do *you* notice? What do *you* think? You could say, 'To add on, I also notice . . .'

"Of course, the reason to notice details is to grow knowledge about the topic, so you need to also say, 'I'm learning that . . .'"

Call for the next partner to also read aloud a text, share observations, and talk about the text.

After Partner 1 had read for awhile, I suggested Partner 2 take a turn to read aloud and share observations.

Remind children that as nonfiction readers they'll see texts everywhere. Recruit them to read attentively while they are at home.

"Readers, the work you did today in school is work you can do tonight at home as well. Right now, think about your house. Are there are places in your house where you can read, noticing the details and really thinking in a way that helps you learn? Do any of you have things to read on your refrigerator door or in a kitchen drawer?"

I added, "I think you'll find that there are more things to read than you might realize. Let me show you what I mean." I distributed some cereal boxes to clusters of children throughout the meeting area. "With the kids near you, read the details, read thoughtfully, saying 'I notice . . .' and then see if you can grow some knowledge together. Think together. Go!"

FIG. 1–3   Partnerships talk and grow knowledge.

Nonfiction Readers Notice, Learn, *and* Question

IN THIS SESSION, you'll teach children that as nonfiction readers notice details and put them together to learn about a topic, they find that questions come up.

GETTING READY

✔ Collect pennies (one for each student or partnership) to study and read. You'll distribute them at the beginning of today's session (see Connection).

✔ Display the "Nonfiction Readers Grow Knowledge" anchor chart begun in Session 1, with a new strategy—"Ask questions."—ready to add (see Connection and Link).

✔ Reuse the enlarged chart from the demonstration book. We use the castle from *Knights in Shining Armor*, by Gail Gibbons (see Teaching).

✔ Distribute the collection of texts and objects from Session 1 for students to study and question (see Active Engagement).

✔ Make available leveled nonfiction books in bins. The books should be highly engaging and cover a variety of topics.

✔ Make sure to have a book baggie for each child so readers are ready to shop for their own books (see Share).

✔ Provide a copy of the reading log for each child (see Share).

MINILESSON

CONNECTION

Remind readers that they learned yesterday to notice details and think about how to put together knowledge about the topic while they read.

"Readers, this morning, I heard about reading work you did last night at home. Tony read his family's mail—it wasn't opened yet, but he could still read the envelopes and learn a lot. His family gets a lot of different kinds of mail! Tony didn't just read the words on all those envelopes. He also did a lot of brainy thinking. How many of you have realized that nonfiction reading involves not only reading the words but also doing a *lot* of thinking?" Lots of children signaled that they'd learned that.

"Last night, I told my friend about your ability to pay close attention, reading in a way that lets you notice things and to think a lot. I bragged to my friend that you are so *brainy* as readers that you could probably read a *penny* and get a lot of knowledge from it."

Distribute a new text—a penny—to study.

"I'm hoping I wasn't exaggerating. Do you think you *could* use all that you learned yesterday to get a lot of knowledge from a penny? Do you?" Kids nodded. Gesturing to yesterday's chart, I listed the points across my fingers.

Nonfiction Readers Grow Knowledge

- Pay attention to details.
- Put the parts of the text together in your mind.

You'll want to decide whether to give a penny to each child instead of each partnership. It's not easy to hold a penny between two people and read together, but on the other hand the point is made even if the penny is shared.

I distributed pennies into cupped hands and said, "You ready? Go!" As children worked in pairs, I listened.

❖ **Name the teaching point.**

"Today I want to teach you that as readers notice details and try putting things together to learn about a topic, *questions* often come up. Readers keep those questions in mind as they read."

TEACHING

Note that some of the children generated questions while reading the penny.

"I noticed that when you read the penny, many of you not only noticed details, putting what you noticed together to learn some things, but you *also* asked questions. When you saw a man's face on the penny, did any of you ask, 'Whose face is that? Why is it here?' That's what readers do. They notice, they learn, and they question."

Return to the diagram from the previous session and model how noticing details and putting those details together can prompt the reader to ask questions.

"Let's read our diagram of the castle again," I said. "Let's reread, noticing and putting what we notice together to learn about castles." I projected the chart of the castle we studied yesterday and began rereading.

I gave children a moment to do this. I voiced over, "Yesterday we noticed this," and I pointed to the moat, "and these," and I pointed to holes in the walls, presumably designed for shooting out arrows. "We put what we saw together and developed the knowledge that castles have a lot of ways to protect people. That work—the work we did yesterday—is what nonfiction readers do; they try to put things together in their minds.

"*Now*, let's reread and see if questions come to mind." I reread the diagram, and this time generated related questions: "Why were they—the people inside—in such danger? Who was trying to get inside the castle? That's what I wonder. Were you wondering that?

"You know what else I'm wondering? I get how the *outside* of the castle tries to protect people, but does the *inside* of the castle protect people too? I'm going to look at this diagram more closely to see if I can figure out if the inside of the castle protects people too.

FIG. 2–1 Distribute pennies to each student or to each partnership.

"Are you starting to have questions, too, about this diagram? I'm sure you are. Do you see how noticing the details *and* raising questions helps us grow more knowledge about our topic, castles?"

ACTIVE ENGAGEMENT

Channel students to revisit the topic they studied in yesterday's minilesson, this time paying special attention to the questions that surface as they grow their knowledge.

"Readers, will you get into your quadrant groups again? And I'm going to distribute the same texts that you read yesterday. Today, begin by doing the work you did yesterday. Read, noticing details, specifics, saying 'I notice . . .' Try to put together what you notice to make knowledge about your topic, and this time, let questions, musings, come to mind as well."

As the children worked, I circled between the groups, voicing over tips and reminders such as these:

"I'm noticing . . ."

"I'm learning . . ."

"I'm wondering . . ."

As children talked, I recorded some of their questions and soon reconvened the class to repeat some of what I'd heard.

LINK

Repeat the teaching point as you send readers off to read.

"Whenever you read nonfiction texts, remember that you read by noticing details, by putting what you notice together to learn about your topic, *and* by asking questions." I added the new strategy to the anchor chart. "Off you go to read your texts!"

You may want to offer a tool to support students as they talk about their thinking. In addition to telling students ways to talk, you might offer a "Ways to Talk about Your Thinking" card, with the prompts written for students to use.

ANCHOR CHART

Nonfiction Readers Grow Knowledge

- Pay attention to details.
- Put the parts of the text together in your mind.
- **Ask questions.**

Ask questions

FIG. 2–2 Ways to Talk about Your Thinking cards.

Celebrating the Nonfiction Reading Skills Your Children Bring

AT THE START OF READING TIME TODAY, your students will be reading the materials—charts, diagrams, brochures, pennies—in their bins, and your goal during this time will be to help them make a lot of meaning out of relatively small amounts of print. Nudge them to thoughtfully notice the smallest of details, putting the information together to construct knowledge. You'll also want to support children in the process of being curious about the information they see, asking and answering questions that will help set them up to construct even more knowledge. You might conduct quick "dip in, dip out" conferences, offering lean prompts such as "What do you notice? Why might it be that way? What does it make you think? What does it make you wonder?" The key to any one of those questions is that you ask it with commitment, not throwing all those questions out at a rat-tat-tat clip, and that you listen intently to the reader's response and extend it.

As you confer with kids who are reading from their bins—full of charts, diagrams, and so on—remember to notice and admire whenever a reader does something you want to support. Dr. Spock's advice on child rearing pertains to your teaching as well: "Catch your kids in the act of doing good," he says. Once you distribute nonfiction books to your kids (midway through today's workshop), you'll see that reading becomes harder for your kids. Many of them may get a bit mired down in those books, struggling with the challenges that nonfiction poses, so for now, build your students' self-concepts as nonfiction readers by celebrating what they do when reading nonfiction texts—even those that contain few words.

For example, you will see some children rereading what they read yesterday. Celebrate this: "I'm seeing that you are going back to the same text. Are you rereading it again, this time looking for the questions you have?" The youngster is apt to say yes, because that is the work you have set the class up to do. "That's a *big* deal—developing the habit of rereading! It's so important. Most people go through life reading only one way—forward—but not you." You could add, "Rereading can help a person put all the parts, all the specifics, together so the reader comes up with a big idea or a big understanding. Is your rereading helping you know or understand something about your topic?"

Of course, once students are reading books, after the mid-workshop teaching point, the work readers are doing will alter a bit, and the things you celebrate will also change. For example, if you see a child read the table of contents, celebrate. If you see a child look back to something that was read earlier, celebrate. You'll find lots of reasons to say, "I'm glad that we're at the start of a nonfiction unit, because I can tell that this unit really brings out the best in you! It's like you are a born nonfiction reader!"

Don't worry that children aren't all that great just yet. Celebrating the strengths they bring to the table is the very best way to accentuate those strengths.

MID-WORKSHOP TEACHING
Extending the Work of Nonfiction Reading to Books

"Readers, let me have your eyes," I said as I held up three books in my hands. "At your tables I have placed bins of just-right nonfiction books! Just like you've been studying and thinking carefully about your maps, diagrams, and directions, noticing all the details and raising questions about them, you can do the same thing with the books that you read! Doing these same things in books will help you to grow . . . *knowledge*! For the next fifteen minutes, will you choose a book and read it in this careful and thoughtful way? When you finish, you can either reread the book or pick another just-right book from the bin near you!"

Encouraging Students to Notice and Wonder Even More

Channel partners to share what they noticed in and learned from a text and to pose questions, helping each other notice, wonder, and say more.

"Readers, stay where you are for our share today, because you'll be working with your partner most of the time. Yesterday you learned that 'It takes two to read.' How many of you found that when you *and* your partner both read a text together, you noticed more and thought more?

"Today when you do this, I know you'll generate questions, too.

"So, Partner 2, will you share your book with Partner 1? Find the part that you want to read a bit of and talk about. Just like before, say, 'I noticed . . . and I *also* noticed . . .' Partner 1 will chime in, perhaps saying, 'I *also* notice . . .'

"Partner 1, will you give me a thumbs up? I have a special job for you. You and your partner will want to talk not only about what you *notice* but also about what you *wonder*. And that takes real thinking. It isn't easy to raise questions. When you do this, you end up having to come up with possible answers, to say things like, 'Maybe . . .' Your job is to get your partner to say more, more, and more."

As readers began working, I stopped everyone to voice over, "When your partner says just a little bit, show your partner that you want to hear more. Gesture like this." I modeled, rolling my hand, much like my mother used to do to me when she was trying to get me to "come along." "Try it!" The children assigned to the listener roles did this. Then I signaled for the conversations to continue.

"Readers, I think you are ready to fill up your book baggies with lots of great topics about which you want to become knowledgeable. Will you go back to your bins of books and choose a whole *bunch* of books that you are interested in reading? And get a brand new reading log to go along with your new book baggie. You'll want to keep a record of your reading life. By the end of the week, you will have read them all. That way you will grow *a lot* of knowledge about the world!"

Reading Log					
Name:					
Date	School/ Home	Title		Minutes	Parent's initials

FIG. 2–3   A new log for the new unit

Session 3

Nonfiction Readers Ask, "What Is This Book Teaching Me?"

MINILESSON

CONNECTION

Name the context for today's lesson: kids have just gotten baggies full of nonfiction books, and they're eager to zoom through them all.

After directing students to come to the meeting area with *one* of the books from their baggie and to sit on the book, I said, "Readers, back at your seats, you each have a baggie *full* of books. When you look at those baggies, you will probably feel like a kid at a candy store. You probably want to gulp all the books down right now, to read one and then the next and then the next, reading on and on and on until you are done."

"After all, the nonfiction books in your baggies are *full* of so many cool facts and features. But remember, just like candy—gulping too much of it too quickly can give you a bellyache—gulping too many books too quickly can give you a . . ." I trailed off, thinking of the just right comparison to make. "A brain-ache!"

I put my hand on my head and squinted my eyes to show how painful a brain-ache can be. The kids giggled. "It's like you get information overload," I said, making my hands pulsate above my head. There was more giggling.

"You need to *savor* your books. Don't just gulp your books down and try to read one after the other. Read closely and carefully, the exact same way you've been reading, noticing, thinking, and questioning the charts, the diagrams, and the pennies," I said and turned the page of an imaginary book, "and then do all that some more, because that is exactly the way nonfiction readers read books, too."

IN THIS SESSION, you'll teach children that nonfiction readers grow their knowledge by putting together the details they read with their own thoughts and asking, "What is this book teaching me?"

GETTING READY

✔ Plan to have students choose one book from their baggie to bring to the meeting area (see Connection).

✔ Make sure you have the demonstration text from Sessions 1 and 2 handy. We use *Knights in Shining Armor*, by Gail Gibbons (see Teaching and Active Engagement).

✔ Display the "Nonfiction Readers Grow Knowledge" chart and have today's strategy—"Think, 'What is this book (and this part) teaching me?'"—ready to add (see Active Engagement and Link).

✔ Ask students to bring one book from their book baggie to get started in the minilesson (see Link).

✔ Refer to the "Readers GROW Like Beanstalks" anchor chart from Unit 1 (see Mid-Workshop Teaching).

❖ **Name the teaching point.**

"Today I want to teach you that to grow knowledge from books, nonfiction readers put what they see and think together and then ask, 'What is this book teaching me?'"

TEACHING

Demonstrate how readers preview a text, noticing and questioning what they see and then thinking about what each part of the book will teach.

"Let's read some parts of *Knights in Shining Armor* together. Let's *not* wait until the end of the book to figure out what the book is teaching us. Just like we did in the first unit, we can take a sneak peek! Look at the different parts of the book to see what they will teach you. For example, we can look at the front and back covers to ask ourselves, 'What will this book teach me?'"

I flipped to the back cover only to see a helmet and an eagle. "Hmm . . . , a helmet. What are helmets used for? Protection during a battle. What will this book teach us? Maybe about battles? Let's look at the front cover." I pointed to the two knights there and said, "I see here that there are two knights and that they are each riding on a horse. They each have a sword, and they seem to be protecting a castle. I think we have already learned that knights ride horses and that they use swords, as well as armor, to protect themselves. So, let me ask, 'What will this book teach us?' I bet this book will teach us even *more* ways that knights protect castles. Do you agree with me?

"Did you see how I used the front and the back covers not just to notice and question but to begin thinking, 'What is this book teaching me?' The front and back covers are important parts of the book. Now we know even more things about knights and castles!"

ACTIVE ENGAGEMENT

Set readers up to carry the question "What is this book teaching me?" in their minds as they begin reading.

"Let's do this with the book we just started reading together and make sure we don't wait until the end to think about the book. Let's stop and think, 'What is this book teaching?' I put my finger at the start of page 14, gesturing for the class to listen in and think along with me.

Just before turning the page I thought aloud, "Let's not wait to let this book teach us more!" I pointed to the first two bullets on the "Nonfiction Readers Grow Knowledge" chart. "Let's pay attention to the details and put them together to think about what this book is teaching." I moved my finger across the page, pointing out things that I anticipated students would not notice.

Of course, it wouldn't be the worst thing in the world for readers to do as they are tempted, to fly through those books, as long as they return to reread them. But too many kids fly through books without a thought—so that when you ask, afterward, what the book was about, they have no clue. And they do that with no intention to reread. That is why we talk up the importance of digesting the content of a book as you read. This is the focus also of the first bend in the first-grade fall nonfiction reading unit.

If you have already introduced Knights in Shining Armor *during read-aloud, ask children to recall what they did to take a sneak peek and to share what they already know about the book.*

It will help the children in your classroom immensely to build a repertoire of skills if you continuously reference past teaching.

Whether you choose this part of the book or a different one for your demonstration, it will work best if the part is unfamiliar to the students.

I said, "Look at the parts of the page. There are two pictures: one shows a knight's face and his clothes." I traced my finger over the picture on page 14, pointing out the helmet, the shield, and the tunic, and then I moved my finger to page 15 and continued speaking. "The other shows the knight inside a suit of armor." I moved my finger around the page to show the differences. "Hmm, . . . what's this part of the book teaching? What are we getting ready to learn? Let's keep studying," I continued. "On this page," I moved my finger back to page 14, "I see that the knight is *inside*. See the window showing outside? He's inside the castle. And on this page," I moved my finger back to page 15, "I see that the knight is *outside*. He's standing in the grass under the blue sky."

Channel students to turn and talk about what the book is teaching, and highlight examples of readers using thinking to grow their knowledge.

"When you have noticed some things and have thought, 'What is this book teaching?' put your thumb on your knee." Thumbs went up, so I immediately said, "Now, turn and talk to your partner about what you think."

I circulated, listening in to partnerships about the details they noticed, before stopping to rearticulate a few. "I heard someone say that the pages show different ways knights dressed—what they wore when they were inside the castle and how they dressed to protect themselves when outside the castle walls. They noticed that the knight in full armor isn't inside the castle courtyard, but that he is out in the open field.

"Interesting! Some of you were discussing the different labels on the page, naming all the different parts of the knight's clothing and uniform. You were questioning the book, and you were noticing that the knight had a shield in both pictures, even when he was inside the castle.

"So what do you think this part is teaching us? Quick, talk to your partner." After listening in to several thinkers, I stopped the class and said, "I heard someone say that this part would probably teach us about how knights dressed and why they wore the things they wore—to protect themselves and others. Thumbs up if you were thinking this, too!" Thumbs were wagging.

"Someone else said that it is teaching us how even when a knight was inside, he had protection: he wore a helmet and kept his sword and shield with him. She even noticed the little weapons on the backs of his shoes—look!" I said and pointed to the spur on the back of the knight's shoe. "Like knights were always—*always*—ready to protect themselves. It must have been very dangerous back then.

"You're totally getting the idea!" I smiled. "You aren't waiting until the very end of the book to figure out what this book is teaching you; you're thinking about that right from the start of reading! That's important work for readers of nonfiction to do as they read their books, so that they grow even *more* knowledge."

Students are offered multiple opportunities to turn and talk during the active engagement. The first turn-and-talk is to give readers time to name details they notice, the second time is to push students to talk about what they are learning from the text.

Even if your students' responses aren't this detailed, you can add in a few details of your own to demonstrate the kind of thinking you hope your students will strive toward.

LINK

Remind children that readers continually think about what a part, a page, or a book is teaching.

"Readers, I added this important work to our chart. After this, always remember that readers don't wait until the end of a book to think! They are *always* thinking, 'What is this part, this page, this book, teaching me?'

"And guess what? Paying attention to details and putting the parts together," I said, pointing to those items on the anchor chart and adding the new strategy, "helps readers answer the question, 'What is this book (and this part) teaching me?'"

> **ANCHOR CHART**
>
> Nonfiction Readers Grow Knowledge
>
> - Pay attention to details.
> - Put the parts of the text together in your mind.
> - Ask questions.
> - **Think, "What is this book (and this part) teaching me?"**

Think, "What is this book (and this part) teaching me?"

Highlight the importance of today's strategy, making sure to add it to the class anchor chart. You'll encourage students to head off, right away, to practice this strategy as they transition to independent reading time.

"Right now, take out the book that you brought to the meeting area and get started. I'm going to float around quickly to remind you to stop and think about that question: 'What is this book teaching?' or 'What is this *part* teaching me?'"

As students pulled their books out from under them, I noticed those who weren't lingering over their front covers and did a voiceover: "Before you even open your books, what are you going to do?"

"Think about what the book is teaching!" several children chimed.

"Don't wait to do that work," I responded. "Take a sneak peek at the front and back covers! Start asking questions even before you open the cover of your book!" As students read, I circulated, voicing over with more scaffolds. When I saw students trying and thinking, I sent them off to their reading spots.

Active Readers Are Thoughtful Readers

Make exemplary behaviors contagious by conducting table compliments.

There is a way in which today will feel like the first day of the unit because suddenly all your kids will have baggies full of nonfiction books and they'll be reading those books silently to themselves, and then during share time, they'll read them aloud to their partners. Hopefully you will have had time between yesterday's share and now to look over the baggies of books, double-checking your children's choices. If last month you recently assessed a reader as able to handle level J books, that reader should have a baggie full of nonfiction books that are either at or easier than level J. In general, nonfiction tends to be a bit harder for most kids, so now is a good time to keep an eye on the effort to match readers to books that are within reach for them.

Since this is the first full day in books, keep the conferring quick, aiming to reach each table. You might conduct a round or two of table compliments, moving quickly from table to table, complimenting readers in replicable ways. You'll want to make contagious the energy of readers whose engagement in reading to grow knowledge is apparent. Compliment readers as you observe them taking sneak peeks, noticing details by reading the *whole* page, accumulating details to consider what each part is teaching, and pausing to consider questions that remain.

Confer to assess and monitor comprehension.

Today's lesson accentuates the lesson you have been trying to bring home since the start of this unit. Readers read *and think*. In fact, reading *is* comprehension. Although you will have taught this by highlighting the positive message, there is also the flip side, which is that readers need to monitor for comprehension and to notice when things aren't making sense. So when they read, asking questions, one question is, "Does that make sense? Am I 'getting' this?" Your readers do need to know when things don't make sense, and they need to know that the first recourse then is to draw on fix-up strategies. In the first unit, readers learned to keep tabs on their comprehension, recognizing moments when they start to read faster and faster, more and more, without *thinking*, so that they can stop and think, "What's happened so far?" You may want

to do some individual conferences, coaching readers to do similar monitoring in their nonfiction books, stopping quickly and often to retell the information they've learned so far. It might be beneficial to turn these interactions into table conferences, reminding all readers that they shouldn't forget to stop, think, and retell as they read—except now they won't be retelling a story but, rather, the information the author is teaching about a particular topic.

> ## MID-WORKSHOP TEACHING
> ### Pausing to Accumulate Knowledge
>
> "Readers, I need your attention for a couple moments," I said as I moved toward the anchor chart and looked out across the room.
>
> "I can feel the buzz in the air as you read and grow knowledge from your books. I see your eyes zoom across the pages of your books, and I see you seeking and finding new bits of information and facts that you didn't know before. Wow, you must feel excited!"
>
> I lowered my voice, "I need you to remember that the work of a nonfiction reader is to grow *knowledge*. So be sure you aren't just zipping through your books—bing, bang, boom! Nonfiction reading isn't about a casual glance," I said, and mimicked how I'd casually look at something.
>
> "Now that you're reading books," I walked toward the "Readers GROW Like Beanstalks" chart and pointed as I said, "keep tabs on your own comprehension. Don't forget to stop and think as you read nonfiction books, too! Just because we are reading a different genre, don't forget to use all the smart work you did to think about your fiction books! Use those same strategies to really think about your reading. Back to it!"

Sharing Newfound Information

Create an opportunity for students to share their newfound information by leading a symphony share.

"Readers, you all are learning about so many topics that I think we should celebrate with a symphony share. Are you game? I'll pretend to be the conductor of a symphony orchestra, and you be the instruments. When I tap my baton toward you, say out loud and clearly some of the interesting things you have learned about the topic you are reading about."

I tapped my baton at one reader, then another, and another. Half a dozen kids called out what they had learned.

"I learned that treasure hunters may have to search for years and years before they find the sunken ship," said Malcolm. My wand moved to Ty. "Some plants trap and kill bugs by turning them into pulp!" he shared. Gasps were heard around the room.

Pausing, I said, "Will each of you *pretend* I just pointed my baton at you and think what *you'd* say? What *have* you learned about from your reading?" They nodded agreement. "Great, turn and tell your partner some of the interesting things you've learned about the topic you're reading about. Partner 2, you'll start today."

Session 4

Nonfiction Readers Ask, "How Does This Book Go?"

MINILESSON

In the connection, you might start by holding up a nonfiction book wrapped with a bow and saying, "I hope you realize that nonfiction books are a gift. You open up a book and—presto—a gift! From one book, you are given the chance to be an expert on butterflies; from another book, the chance to know how bridges are made."

"When I'm given a gift—say, on my birthday—I like to feel the weight of the package even before I unwrap it. I try to figure out what's inside. I turn it one way, another, another, just thinking, 'What's in this package?' Yesterday, you learned that readers do something similar before they open the gift of a nonfiction book. They try to figure out what the book will teach them, what the gift of knowledge will be."

For your teaching point you might say, "Today I want to teach you that when readers get ready to read and learn from a nonfiction book, they preview *all* the different parts of the book when they take a sneak peek. Readers look at each part and think, "How does this book go?"

In your teaching, you can carefully unwrap the bow on the book you displayed during the connection. Then show students the book on the document camera, if one is available, and begin to preview it. You might say to your students, "Will you help me get ready to read this book? To do this, let's look together carefully at each of the parts and think, 'How does this book go? What is this book going to teach me?' Are you ready?"

You might first quickly read the title and then name things you expect to learn about based on the cover of the book. You could model what students will likely do first, just naming the topic, and then show how you push your thinking deeper. "I see a tiger on the front cover, and the title is *Tigers*, so I know this book will teach about tigers." You might pause dramatically before returning to the book and saying, "Wait, let me see if I can push myself further. I've read books about animals before, and I know they often have a chapter about where animals live and another chapter about babies, so I bet those will be in this book."

Turning to the table of contents, you might say, "You can look in the table of contents to see if this book has a chapter about where animals live or one about tiger babies." Continue to flip the pages of the book, pointing out the features that will help the children grow their knowledge as they read, features such as headings and large photographs or pictures. (If you teach from *Units of Study for Information, Opinion, and Narrative Writing*, these text features are referred to as helpers.)

After you have shown students how you preview the book to anticipate the content of it, you can debrief by saying, "Do you see how by studying each part of the text and asking, 'How does this book go?' we got ideas about what this book would teach? You are getting ready to read! You are getting ready to be given the gift of knowledge."

In the active engagement, you may ask partners to take turns setting themselves up for the first book that they will read. Remind them that they want to study each part of the book, and think, "How does this book go? What is this book going to teach me?" You could suggest partners do this work together, with Partner 1 pulling out a book and both partners pouring over it. You will likely want to voice over to keep students moving through this process and ensure they preview all the parts of the text. "Look at the front and back covers first, and think, 'How does this book go?'" Then, say, "Look inside the book. Is there a table of contents? Study it, thinking about how this book goes." Continue coaching students until they have previewed a text.

In the link, you can remind students that they have learned many ways that readers can be sure to receive the gift that nonfiction books give, to read in ways that help them grow knowledge. Referring to the class anchor chart, you could touch each former teaching point (now turned into a bullet on the chart) while channeling students to signal if that particular bullet is something they now do as nonfiction readers whenever they read. Then, you might choose to remind readers of your teaching point—that they now know that previewing a text means more than just looking at the front and back covers, but also looking at all the text features across the book to glean what the book will probably teach about the topic.

The goal is not simply to explore a table of contents, but rather to teach readers the importance of figuring out how a nonfiction text is organized and making plans to learn from the text based on their findings.

CONFERRING AND SMALL-GROUP WORK

As you begin to confer and pull small groups, you will want to support readers with this grown-up method of previewing and predicting before diving into nonfiction reading. In much the same spirit, you could decide to do some text-level introductions as a method of small-group instruction.

You may find that you have a group of readers ready to move up into the next text level and want to introduce this group of like-level readers to a new level. If this is the case, do what you typically do in a guided reading session, and give these students not just a book introduction but an introduction to books at this "new level" of reading. You may have readers beginning to move into levels I/J/K. Readers sometimes have trouble making this jump and may need support to make this move. Many of these not only have many more lines of print per page, but also have more pages in general. With these students, you may decide to do a book introduction that focuses heavily on setting readers up to successfully synthesize information.

Be sure that, as you introduce the book, you emphasize what makes these books more challenging as well as the need to be even more thoughtful and strategic in the thinking work that the children will need to do.

Facilitate a quick sneak peek that gets readers anticipating the big parts of the topic that they'll learn about before they even start reading. Additionally at these levels, there are more polysyllabic words tucked inside complex and compound sentences. This may pose some difficulties for these readers. Consider pointing out a couple of these before children begin to read, and remind them of the word-solving strategies that they'll need to utilize when facing unknown words in any text in this level.

Give the kids the text to read, and stand by for part of the read, offering lean prompts, especially reminding readers to self-monitor to ensure that the words they read sound like they would in a book, make sense, and look right. Self-monitoring is of the utmost importance to readers looking to make this jump—both monitoring to check that the meaning of a text fits with the reader's knowledge, as well as monitoring meaning and knowing when it has broken down and has been lost.

Then you may decide to let the kids read in pairs up to a certain point and then have them return to the group to briefly talk about what they learned. Remind them to keep looking out for and using the things you mentioned in the introduction. Tell them that these are now typical things to find and think about at this new level.

Mid-Workshop Teaching

For your mid-workshop teaching, you might remind students that as they read, they can confirm whether the book does, in fact, teach them what they expected to learn. The greatest part of reading is being surprised, so encourage them to study the pages closely and to think, "Oh, *now* I see how this book goes!"

SHARE

For your share, you may want to point out that sometimes books don't have a lot of text features that can help readers anticipate how the book will go, identifying the topics and subtopics that will be taught in the book. Suggest that the good news is that when readers get together with a partner, that's a good time to say, "Help!" and "I tried this but I had some trouble." Rally partners to do the hard work of orienting themselves to books that don't supply headings and subheadings or other clues that foreshadow the contents of the book. Suggest that after reading a part of a book without text features they might work together to add their own, using Post-it notes to create headings, captions, or labels that will help readers retell what that part just taught them.

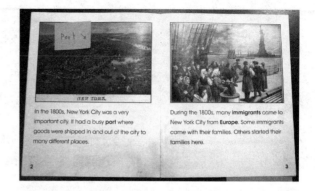

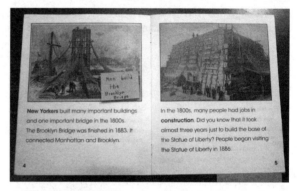

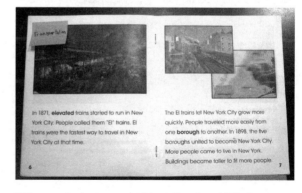

FIG. 4–1 Partners worked together to add their own text features, using Post-it notes to create headings, captions, or labels that will help readers retell what that part just taught them.

Celebrate the Gift of Learning Something New

IN THIS SESSION, you'll close the work of the bend by reminding readers that new information requires special attention.

GETTING READY

✔ Be prepared to instruct children to bring their entire book baggie to the meeting area but to sit on it until the Link (see Connection and Link).

✔ Gift wrap another high-interest nonfiction text, complete with over-the-top ribbons and bows, to give the illusion that a book fairy has visited the classroom (see Connection and Teaching and Active Engagement).

✔ Gather a couple of nonfiction books to hold up as examples (see Connection).

✔ Give students Post-it notes to mark up pages in their books (see Share).

MINILESSON

CONNECTION

Remind students of times when the tooth fairy came—the excitement—and then tell them that, lo and behold, a *book* fairy has visited the classroom.

"Readers, bring your whole book baggie with you and hurry to our meeting area. Come quick as a wink because I need to tell you something exciting." Once the kids had gathered and were sitting on their book baggies, jittery with excitement, I began. "How many of you have ever put a tooth under your pillow and then, in the morning, stuck your hand under the pillow and found that the tooth fairy had been there?" Hands shot up.

"You are not going to believe this, but last night, I think a *book fairy* must have come to our classroom. Because look what was here on my chair when I arrived this morning!" I revealed a beautifully wrapped gift, with a lavish profusion of bows.

"Yesterday we talked about how books are a gift of knowledge. One might give us the knowledge of the saber-toothed tiger," and I held up one book, "and another might explain how to make paper planes," and I held up another book. "Remember that we learned yesterday that readers take a sneak peek at their nonfiction books. I'm thinking we could do that together, with this book. You game?"

I proceeded to reveal first a part of the cover, whereupon, with my encouragement, everyone called out what they surmised the book would teach them. Then I revealed other bits of the book—the full cover, the headings, the pictures. The class predicted together.

"We've got the book all figured out, right? We're pretty sure that we know how the gift of this book will go."

❖ **Name the teaching point.**

"Today I want to teach you that one of the best things about books is that even after you take a sneak peek and you anticipate what the book will probably teach you, there will be surprises. Usually, the places where books surprise you are the places where they teach you the most, so be glad for the surprises."

TEACHING

Emphasize that even after previewing a book, readers are usually surprised. When a reader is surprised, this is often when the reader is learning, outgrowing old knowledge and gaining new knowledge.

I reiterated what the class imagined they'd find inside the covers of our fairy gift book and then said, "After you look over a book, predicting how it will go, after you take a sneak peek, you'll read. One of the fun things about reading is that as you move through a book, you will often think, 'Yep, I knew it!' Sometimes, however, you'll think: '*What?* That's a total surprise!'

We haven't specified the title of the book and only summarize some of the content of this minilesson, because any high-interest nonfiction book that contains interesting new facts within the first page or two will do perfectly.

"Here's the thing. If the information in a nonfiction book is a surprise, this is usually because the information is new to you, so it will change how you think. When you start reading, thinking one thing, and then as you read along, you discover something different so that you change your mind—that is called *learning*. It's just about the best thing in the world!"

After explaining the value of being surprised by the content of a book, recruit kids to read with you, and ask them to note when they are surprised. Those will be the learning moments.

"So, let's read together the book that the book fairy left us. As we read, I'm pretty sure there will be places in the book where the content will surprise us. As we read, if we come to some information that is new to you, some information that surprises you, signal with a thumbs up. If that happens, hopefully it will mean that you can literally feel yourself getting smarter as we read!"

A book fairy delivers the gift of reading.

I read the first few pages in the book. Whenever a thumb went up, I nodded, and in a celebratory way, smiled and pointed to that youngster. Often I signaled that I, too, had just learned something new.

Add on a new tip: after reading a bit, after being surprised several times, it is helpful to pause and recall this new learning, asking "What surprising information did I learn?"

"When you learn new things as you read, it is important to try to remember those things. Sometimes after reading a bit, it helps to pause and think, 'So what surprising new information did I learn?' Just saying the information to yourself, teaching yourself the information, helps you to remember it." I then shared some of my new learning aloud to demonstrate this.

Asking children to participate in your teaching with a simple gesture such as a thumbs up will ensure that students stay engaged and will give them an extra opportunity to give the strategy a try.

ACTIVE ENGAGEMENT

Channel kids to continue reading, remembering to think and put learning together along the way.

I reminded the class about what they had expected to find in the upcoming part of the book fairy's gift-book, and suggested we could read on until we came to surprising new information. "After we've read a bunch of new information, what can we do to make it more likely that we remember that information?" I asked, and some members of the class chimed in that we could pause and teach ourselves the information.

I read on, and after we'd read some new information, I paused. "Did you encounter any surprising new information?" I asked, and when everyone agreed that yes, indeed, the information was new, I said, "So right now, teach yourself what you have learned about our topic. As a way to remember it, I'm going to list what I've learned across my fingers. You can do the same, or find another way to hold on to what you have learned. Then turn and share with your partner what you learned."

LINK

Invite kids to give the gift of knowledge by presenting special books to reading partners.

"Readers, right now, will each partner pretend to be a book fairy? Will you choose one really great book from your own book baggie that you're going to give to your partner? Once you have given your partner a gift book, and your partner has given you one, you can go to your reading spots and get started. You may want to start by reading the gift book. Or you can continue with whatever book you left off reading. But whatever you do, when you go to start a book, even after you take a sneak peek and you anticipate what the book will probably teach you, remember, there will be surprises. Usually, the places where books surprise you are the places where they teach you the most, so be glad for the surprises."

Stepping Back to Research and Check In

Make sure readers are engaged and reading. Then begin conferring with individual students.

There will be days, studding your year, when you decide to step back and check that the fundamentals are in place. You could decide to take a moment to step back from the class and research—at large—to make certain that readers are previewing and preparing to read before diving into their new books.

You will want to glean some idea of how well your students are doing with navigating the texts that they are reading. Are they able to put multiple paragraphs of information together to figure out what the page (or the part) is mostly about? Are they able to fit the individual pages they've read into a coherent and memorable bit of knowledge? Help them use headings and titles to think about the main topics in different parts of the text, and then help them have something to say about each of those topics.

Gather a group of readers who would benefit from coaching around fluency.

You may decide to listen to several readers read their text aloud to you. For example, as your conferring notes will remind you, you may have a few students who received help with fluency earlier in the year. They'll probably still need extra support now that they are in nonfiction texts. You might, for example, pull a small group and work with them on scooping up a bunch of words together.

You might say to this group of students, "As you read your nonfiction texts, you have to make sure that what you read makes sense and sounds right to you. It should sound like someone is reporting to you on important information you need to know."

Lift the level of partnerships by coaching readers during the share.

Lastly, on this day, you may decide to work with a couple of partners. Remember, it is crucial to support students' talk about texts as well as their processing of texts, especially since this is a major way students not only show their understanding but make new understandings together. Listen closely as readers tell you what they are learning about between the pages of their texts.

MID-WORKSHOP TEACHING   **Noticing Where and When Books Change to Teach Something New about a Topic**

"Readers, can I have your eyes up on me," I said as I stood in the middle of the classroom. "I see so many of you stopping because you are surprised. I hear how you are really turning on your thinking! As you do this I have a couple of tips for you. First, as you read along in a new text, be ready to think to yourself, 'Has this book just turned a corner and is now teaching me something quite new?' If so, you will want to make note of that as you are reading.

"Second, you can think about the information you just read and think to yourself, 'Does this new information fit with something earlier in the book?' You can look back and think about how the parts are connected.

"Look at what you are reading right now and ask yourself either, 'Has this book just turned a corner and is teaching me now something totally new?' or 'Does this new information fit with something earlier in the book?' Go ahead and keep reading."

Changing Your Voice to Match the Information Inside Your Texts

Model how students can use their voices to show which parts of the book are important and which parts surprised them.

"Readers, let's get ready to meet with our partners for our share session. Look over what you read today. Find a couple of parts where you were surprised or found some really important or interesting information. First, mark those parts with a Post-it, and then sit with your partner." As soon as all were assembled on the rug, I continued.

"Readers, it must feel great to be able to read and find parts of your books that matter to you. I can tell because of the way I see you've marked up your books, ready to read and talk with your partners. As you read and share those important parts with your partners, try to make sure that you are really trying to use your voice to show the thinking that is on the page."

"Try to read the parts that were surprising to you, in a *surprising* way. Just like we did in our first unit of study this year. Maybe there is a part that is particularly important. Make sure you are trying to use your voice to *show* that it is important." I played with my voice here, trying to emphasize what surprising parts sounded like as well as parts of great importance to readers.

"As you use your voice to read and show your thinking, your partner will be better able to understand what your book is about. Of course, after you read, don't forget to talk about the part together. Then go on to other parts in your book and to other books!"

FIG. 5–1   A reader names his reaction and his understanding by jotting a quick Shocker! Post-it.

Anticipating and Using the Lingo of a Nonfiction Topic

IN THIS SESSION, you'll build context and urgency around the work of the bend, explaining that reading to learn and using vocabulary is an important part of growing knowledge.

GETTING READY

✔ Use highlighter tape to mask several words children will most likely be able to generate when asked to think of topic words to go with the title of the nonfiction book you are going to read together. We use *Tigers*, by Laura Marsh (see Teaching).

✔ Have on hand a place, such as a giant sticky note, to record keywords (see Teaching).

✔ Ask children to bring one book from their book baggies, which should be filled with new books, to the meeting area (see Active Engagement).

✔ Display the "Nonfiction Readers Grow Knowledge" anchor chart and be ready to add the strategy "Understand and use keywords." to the chart (see Link). 👆

✔ Begin a new anchor chart titled "Talk the Talk! Read to Learn the Lingo!" and be ready to add the strategy "Expect and look out for keywords" (see Link). 👆

✔ Make sure students have a book that they have read and from which they can discuss some keywords, possibly the book they used in the active engagement (see Share).

MINILESSON

CONNECTION

Explain that learning about a topic involves understanding the language that explains it. Exemplify this by citing the kids' abilities to talk the lingo of a high-interest topic.

"Readers, my nephew is an expert on skateboarding, and the other day at the park he was teaching me about skateboarding. When he started teaching me, I thought he was speaking in French or something. He said, 'To skateboard, you need to get a classic board and start practicing some rad tricks. You should start by trying to do an ollie. To do an ollie you'll have to get a cling grip on the deck. Ollies are so classic! You can really grab some air. I can kind of do an airwalk grab. One time I think I even did a bail but I fell down and couldn't get it to happen again. You gotta be careful, though. If your bushings are dull then your baseplate will slide and you'll end up in a hopper.'

"I just sat there, with my mouth open, and stared at Troy. Then I said, 'Troy, would you speak in English, 'cause I don't understand French.' He looked at me like I was *nuts* and said, 'I *am* talking in English. I'm talking the talk that a skateboarding expert talks!'

"What I realized is that to grow knowledge about a topic, readers have to talk the talk of that topic by understanding and *using* the keywords that go with it—the lingo. That is true of any topic. To be an expert on basketball, you can't do this," I said and mimed dribbling the basketball, "and say, 'I *bounced* the round ball.' Instead, you need to say . . . what?"

The children chimed in, "Dribbled the basketball!"

"And if you are an expert on basketball, you can't say, 'I threw the ball into the *ring*.'" I paused as I mimed tossing an imaginary ball into the hoop. The children substituted *hoop* for *ring*.

"It's like basketball has its own language. It has its own lingo. And people who know about basketball don't just know how to play the game. They know how to talk the talk by using *lingo* to speak the language of the topic. There are words like *hoop, dribble, foul,* and *court.* And if you want to sound like an expert about basketball, you need to learn to talk the talk by using basketball lingo.

"The thing is—sometimes keywords can be tough to read. You can get stuck over them, so I'm going to help you spend a few days getting stronger at being the kind of readers that learn and use the lingo to talk the talk of different topics."

❖ **Name the teaching point.**

"Today I want to teach you that even before nonfiction readers start to read a new book—one they expect will probably be filled with topic-specific vocabulary—they think, 'What keywords do I expect to run into?' and they generate a little list. Later, when readers encounter one of those words in the book, they don't get as stuck. Instead, they think, 'I *knew* that word would be here!'"

TEACHING

Brainstorm a set of words you're apt to encounter in the book you set out to read, and then read on, getting stuck on a tricky word before realizing it's in your word bank.

Putting a copy of *Tigers* under the document camera, I said, "We're going to pretend that we haven't seen this book before, and let's think of the words we *already* know about this topic. We should try to *talk the talk* of tigers. Then, when we read, we'll notice those keywords and also find new words. Hmm, . . . tigers. What are some keywords that might go with the topic that we already know?" I trailed off a second to allow children time to think alongside me.

"I'm thinking of words like *stripes* and *cubs,*" I said as I jotted the words on a giant sticky note. "What other keywords might we run into? I see some of you have thoughts. See if our thinking matches. Are we trying to speak the same lingo of our book? I am thinking *fur.* And maybe *hunters.*" I added both words to my word bank. "Did you think about those words, too? Are there others?" I fielded a couple of responses.

Jungle, paws, animals, and *dangerous* popcorned from around the room as I added them to the list.

"Wow, it seems like we are really getting into our *Tigers* book. We're anticipating the keywords we might meet inside the book. We are talking the talk of the topic by thinking about the lingo before we even start reading."

Be sure to practice the "lingo" that goes with your example so that when you deliver it to students, the key vocabulary words pop out and get students' attention.

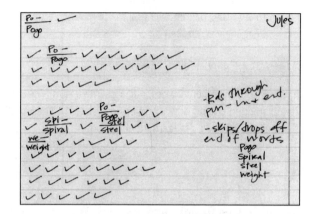

FIG. 6–1   Informal Running Record showing a student who reads through unknown words without attempting to check for accuracy or make meaning

FIG. 6–2   A teacher jots students' responses as they generate topic-specific vocabulary.

If you know your minilessons tend to run long, you might simply ask students to think of some words silently and then name a few aloud yourself to keep things moving.

Shift to reading aloud with the children, knowing that the work you and they just did, brainstorming vocabulary words, will prepare them to read those words with more ease.

"Now as we read, we may be very likely to run into some of these keywords, and when we do, we can say, 'Aha! We've been expecting you! We *knew* you would be in this book!'" I opened the book to page 5 and, projecting the book, began to lead the children in choral reading. When we came to the word *animals*, which I had covered with highlighter tape earlier, my voice trailed off.

> *Tigers are big and beautiful . . .*

I paused on the covered word, stalling. "Wait a minute! Is this one of the keywords we expected to see? Animals!" Heads nodded up and down, and I said, "Aha! We knew you'd be in this book! Now we can use this key word to really think about what we are learning about tigers."

ACTIVE ENGAGEMENT

Set children up to anticipate keywords in new books, and then coach in as they read on the lookout for the keywords.

"It's time to try this in your own book—for real, with a brand new text! Get ready to talk the talk of your new book by thinking about what keywords you'll probably meet inside the book. Partner 1, will you take out that brand new book you brought with you and try this work with Partner 2's help? Put that one book right between you and Partner 2. Read the title together and think about the topic of the book."

All the Partner 1s placed a book in the middle of their partnership, and I continued, "Think about the *lingo* that you'll meet inside your book. Try to *talk the talk* of your topic. Say the keywords you think you'll meet when you start reading. Partner 2, don't be shy! Don't just sit and listen to Partner 1 talk that talk. If *you* know any keywords—any lingo—that could help your partner read and learn about the book, add your thinking into the mix! Get to it! Pip pip!"

I circulated for a minute or two, coaching kids as they anticipated keywords that went with the topics of their books. After a moment, I interrupted the talkers and said, "Now, begin to read just the first part of your book together, and be on the lookout for the keywords, the lingo you've already expected to see—especially if you get stuck, because the words you expected to meet in the book might be there to help you."

As readers worked together to read and navigate the first several pages of their new texts, there were squeals and happy clapping when, in just the first few pages of the book, they came upon words they were expecting to meet. Each time I heard a confirmation, I made a point to coach in and add, "Those keywords are helping you *talk the talk* right from the start!"

Prior to the start of today's lesson, you will want to strategically cover words with highlighter tape throughout your demonstration text. We suggest that you cover words that students will be able to generate when asked to think about keywords that go with the topic of the book. Here, I covered the word animals *in advance so that I could model getting stuck on the word before solving it.*

FIG. 6–3 Students' predictions for "words they will meet" inside new nonfiction texts

LINK

Reconvene readers to restate the teaching point and name the ambitious work that lies ahead in this bend.

"Readers, I can hear and see that you are starting to anticipate the keywords you'll find when you read your new books. Not only are you preparing to talk the talk and use the lingo of your topics, but you are growing knowledge about a topic right away. You aren't letting those words get you stuck; you are prepared to see them! You spot them and you say, 'Aha! I knew you'd be here! Let me learn all about you!' before reading the word and reading on."

Begin a chart that will grow to support the ambitious work of the second bend.

First, I pointed to the anchor chart from the first bend, to which I had added a new strategy. I said, "Readers, understanding keywords is a super important part of reading to grow knowledge."

ANCHOR CHART

Nonfiction Readers Grow Knowledge

- Pay attention to details.
- Put the parts of the text together in your mind.
- Ask questions.
- Think, "What is this book (and this part) teaching me?"
- **Understand and use keywords.**

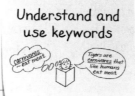

Understand and use keywords

"This can be challenging work! Let's start a new chart to help you remember the ways you can learn the *lingo* of your books so that you can keep growing knowledge by talking the talk of your topics. I gestured to the new anchor chart and the first strategy:

"Just like Troy can do with skateboarding, just like what *we* started to do with tigers, and *you* are starting to do with the books you brought, you're getting ready to talk the talk of your books, to *use* and understand the lingo. You're asking yourself, 'What keywords will I probably run into?' Then, when you encounter those words, don't get stuck on them. Instead think, 'Oh yes, there's that word! Aha! I knew it would be here!' And read on!"

ANCHOR CHART

Talk the Talk! Read to Learn the Lingo!

- **Expect and look out for keywords.**

Beginning the Work of the New Bend

Get the new work going in the beginning of this new bend.

As your readers set off on the first day of this new bend, excited and engaged in learning not only about their books but also focusing on the specialized vocabulary and language their books will teach, you'll have the opportunity to pull small groups and do spot checks on nonfiction reading comprehension.

As you move from table to table, listen in to individual students and the lingo they are finding. Spread the excitement of thinking about and finding words to the rest of the students at a table. You might say, "Readers, John was expecting to find *tadpoles*, *hibernate*, and *pond* in his book about frogs. He has found *pond* and *tadpoles* so far! Have you checked your list of the words and lingo you thought you were going to find? Have you found any? Or discovered new ones? Look now. I'll come around and coach you to find some more. Keep reading!"

Design a series of small groups that you will be able to pull and teach across the next couple of weeks.

Certainly, when you look across your notes from last week, and when you listen in to your readers, you will want to start a couple of small groups to support your readers' comprehension. Look to see who may need support in paying closer attention to the details in the text and monitoring for meaning as they read. Look to see who may need more support in putting together the parts of their texts to grow new knowledge.

Pull each of these groups for five to ten minutes to have the students work on this in their just-right book. Say to the readers, "As you are reading, don't let the details of the text fly by you. Think about what you are reading. Remember that you ask a question, think about what this is teaching you, or look at the picture and think about what is happening. Let's do that in our own books with a partner first. Partner 1 will read and then both of you will read and talk about the details on the page. You can try any of these things to help you. I will listen in and help you say more about what you see, notice, and think."

Then you will want to listen and prompt students, giving directions and restating the teaching point, to support students in trying the work several times in their books. You may reconvene this group the next day, providing less scaffolding. See Session 7 for a suggestion of the next thing you may want to do with this type of small group.

MID-WORKSHOP TEACHING
Saying *and* Understanding Keywords

"Readers, I have a rather big announcement to make," I said with a dramatic pause, while standing in the middle of the classroom. "I see you looking and finding keywords in your books. Getting ready to meet some of those keywords is really helping you to zip through your books.

"Here's the thing—and it's a bit of a sticky wicket. Some of you are skipping over some of your words because they seem 'easy.' When you read keywords—even if they are words you *know* you know—don't just read right over them and keep going. Stop. Make sure you understand what the word means. You have to be the person who checks in with yourself to make sure you're understanding what the word says—and what the word means— even when the key word is easy to read. You need to ask yourself, 'What does this word mean?' and '*How* is this word important to the topic?' Take time to work it out in your brain before you zip on to the next part of your text. Now, back to your own reading."

Using Keywords to Talk the Talk Together

Set partners up to share and speak the lingo of their books.

"Readers, you have been talking the talk of your topics! You aren't just reading to grow knowledge. You're learning the lingo, too. We have people learning the lingo of frogs and their life cycle, of plants—whoops! Let me use the lingo—*botany*—and even talking the talk of race cars! Thinking about the keywords that go with a topic not only sets you up before you read but also helps you *after* you read. You can use those words to think about your topic and speak its language.

"So let's set up topic conversations. Partner 2, talk the talk about your topic and use as many of your keywords as you can. *Really* use the lingo of your topic. Don't forget that you can use your book to go back and give your memory a little jog to remember the words you expected and saw inside your books.

"Partner 1, your job isn't just to sit by and—ho-hum—listen. Your job is to listen closely and learn from your partner and her reading. Is she using the *lingo* of her book to speak the topic's language? Does the lingo she's using help *you* learn? Learning the lingo of a topic can be tough! Remember how it felt to me like my nephew was speaking in an entirely different language about skateboards? So ask questions if you need to, like, 'I'm not sure what you mean. Can you say more?' or 'What does that thing really do?' or 'I don't really understand. Can you give me an example?'"

FIG. 6–4 Partnerships talking the talk of their nonfiction texts.

Using Text Features to Notice and Understand Keywords

IN THIS SESSION, you'll teach children to notice and utilize text features when figuring out keywords.

GETTING READY

✔ Display the anchor chart "Talk the Talk! Read to Learn the Lingo!" and be ready to add the strategy "Look for and use features to help." (see Connection and Active Engagement).

✔ Use your demonstration text to highlight keywords supported in text features. We use *Tigers*, by Laura Marsh, and we covered the words *camouflage* and *prey* with highlighter tape (see Teaching and Active Engagement).

✔ Select a text with vocabulary-related text features (e.g., text box, boldface words, glossary) to support an inquiry into text features (see Share).

✔ Make sure children have their book baggies with them and access to Post-its and pencils to spotlight a keyword that isn't supported in a feature (see Share).

MINILESSON

CONNECTION

Celebrate the way readers have embraced the work of learning and using topic vocabulary before warning them that inevitable challenges lie ahead.

"Isn't it amazing how in just one day we all started speaking new languages?" I questioned as the kids sat down in their rug spots. I got a couple of funny looks, so I pointed to the new anchor chart and said, "You did! *You* started to talk the talk as you read to learn the lingo of different topics! Some of you ran into some hard words that seemed tricky and sticky at first, but then you took a deep breath, thought about the words you expected to find in a book, and realized you were stuck on one of those words!

"Friends, I'm not going to sugarcoat it for you. It wasn't always easy work." I paused—even more dramatically than normally. "There were times when, try as you might, you couldn't figure out a keyword. You could see it. You could say it. You even thought you *might* know what it meant. But you couldn't be absolutely sure. There's something you need to know," I said leaning in close.

"The authors of information books want to help you talk the talk! There are keywords that they want to make sure you know, so they spotlight them in helpful features. These features help you learn the lingo of your topic. It's almost as if the author is saying, 'Hey! *This* is a keyword, and I want to help you learn it!'"

❖ **Name the teaching point.**

"Today I want to teach you that nonfiction readers find keywords and work to know what those keywords mean. Readers can find, and sometimes learn about, keywords from reading the boldface words, the text boxes, the labels, the glossaries—the works! When readers learn more about a keyword, they learn more about the topic."

TEACHING

Recruit the kids to join you in continuing the class book, this time encountering a domain-specific term in a sentence and searching for help from the rest of the page, then finding it in a text box.

I placed *Tigers*, by Laura Marsh, on the document camera, turned to page 8, and said, "Let's keep reading to learn the lingo so that we can talk the tiger talk. Look out for keywords that Laura Marsh spotlights, letting us know we should learn more about them. Let's read together. When you spot a keyword, think, 'Are there text features on the page that help me understand the word (and the topic) better?'"

> *Built for Hunting*
>
> *Tigers are fierce hunters. Their bodies are built for catching prey.*

"I think *prey* seems like a key word here. If you already know this word, put your thumb on your knee. Okay, some of you do and some of you don't. Let's see if Laura Marsh gives us any help. Did she spotlight the word in a text feature?"

I scanned the pages quickly with my finger, stopping at a text box at the bottom of page 9. "Look!" I pointed to the "Tiger Term" text box and slid the book back under the document camera. "That word, *prey*! It's here, inside this text box! Let's use the text feature to learn about *prey*. Let's read!"

> *Prey: An animal that is eaten by another animal.*

"Hmm, . . . so the word *prey* refers to an animal that other animals eat as food. Is that what you thought the term meant? Now you know! The author helped us learn the tiger talk by putting the definition in this special box."

Channel the kids to reread with the definition in mind, noting how much clarity they gain from understanding the key term.

"Okay, let's reread, now that we know what *prey* means." We reread the text and I said, "So tigers are built for catching prey. They are so big and strong that they can catch bigger kinds of prey to eat. That makes total sense. And wasn't it helpful of the author to help us understand the keyword, *prey*?"

ACTIVE ENGAGEMENT

Ask children to read on, this time reading in partnerships, helping each other locate and come to understand any additional keywords they encounter.

"As you and your partner read on, be on the lookout for more keywords, and if you find one, look to see if the author has included a text feature that can help you understand that word while also growing knowledge about the topic." I then displayed page 8 and signaled for children to read it to each other, not in whole-class unison.

It is next to impossible to find keywords that are unknown to all readers. You'll notice we choose several words in hopes that some of the keywords are new to the class.

Coat: A tiger's stripes camouflage it in tall grass and dry leaves. Its prey may not see the tiger until it's too late.

I listened to children talking together. "I love that you are really working to figure out the hard word!" I said, knowing that *camouflage* would pose challenges for them. "Even if you think you know what this means, look to see if the author has provided more information in one of the text features." I added the new strategy to the growing chart.

LINK

Remind readers of the main point of the minilesson—that reading to learn about a topic involves learning the keywords, and sometimes the author provides some help.

"Readers, today I hope you have learned that it is really helpful to watch for keywords when you are reading to learn about a topic. If you find a word that you think is important to the topic—like *prey* and *camouflage* are important to tigers—chances are good that the author will help you understand those words. "The important thing is that when you understand a keyword, you understand something key about your topic."

Challenge readers to begin reading time today not with reading onward, but with returning to a book they have already read, this time revisiting it with the lens of looking for keywords and seeking to understand them.

"I know you are dying to get started reading your nonfiction books, but before you do that, will you return to a book you have already read that is in your baggie, and this time will you look back at that book to notice whether there are keywords there that you missed? Go on a scavenger hunt through that book, noticing all the keywords. When you find one, look to see if the author has actually helped you understand that word. You might find that help in a text box or a glossary or—well, you look and see! Go to it!"

I waited a few moments as kids read through their books, skimming and scanning, looking for bold words, text boxes, labels, captions, glossaries, and indexes. I heard a buzz of, "I found a bold word!" "Mine had a text box too!" and "Mine has a glossary!"

"Wow, you are lucky that the authors of your books gave you all that help! Not *all* authors of nonfiction books provide you with this sort of help, but when they do, you can cheer, 'Yes! Thank you, author!' Use those features as you read!"

Don't worry too much about how your English language learners will participate in this activity. Ensure that they have a level of support that coincides with their language proficiency. This interactive work with their peers will contribute in a positive way to their language development. Remember, sometimes peer-speak is better received than teacher-speak, so trust the language learning process.

You may want to leave a few extra moments during the link and have students begin reading and finding key vocabulary so you can move around and support readers as needed.

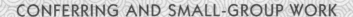

Building Students' Ability to Work Independently

Lead follow-up small-group strategy lessons started at the beginning of the bend and release some of the scaffolding to let students work with more independence.

Prior to today, you have most likely taught strategy lessons to one or more small groups. You may have taught them to pay closer attention to details or to put parts of the text together to grow an understanding of the main topic. Either way, it is always important for you to lead follow-up lessons so that the work you begin is supported across time. One important thing is that as you meet with each group again (and again), you can lessen the amount of scaffolding you provide. For example, if you first led a heavily scaffolded group, the next time you may channel students to work with each other in pairs, allowing students to receive partner support instead of your support.

When you meet with a group today, for about ten minutes, you might start by saying, "Yesterday you tried this out with a partner, and today you will try it on your own. You will read in your minds, and then I will tap you, gently, on the arm. I will ask you to share your thinking with me about that page and work. I may have you read a bit to me as well, before I coach you, and then I will have you continue the work in your head. Ready?"

Start a guided reading group (or two) with readers who may be ready to move up a level.

You will want to see which students are ready to work on more challenging texts. Study your running records and your conferring notes, looking to see which students are integrating sources of information and require more demanding texts. You might target kids who have only a couple of goals to work on in new texts. These students might not need very heavy scaffolding to move into the next text level. They might just need a series of book introductions to support their reading, with hardly any coaching of challenging concepts, phrases, structure, or vocabulary.

MID-WORKSHOP TEACHING   **Learning about Glossaries**

"Readers, can I have your eyes and ears and attention!" I said, standing in the middle of the room.

"The work you are doing—collecting keywords that go with a book and a topic—makes me think you are almost writing *glossaries* for the book you are reading! You could almost call the author up on the phone and say 'Hey, Mr. Author! I've written a glossary for your book. You want to add it to your book the next time you make new copies?'

"If the author wants to add your list of keywords as a glossary in the book, where will that glossary go? Can you and your partner point to the places in the books you are reading now where the author might print your list of keywords?"

Some children turned to the back of their book, and I called on one of them to stand and show everyone. A few kids said, "My book already has a glossary at the back," and I pointed that out as well.

Then I said, "Look through your baggies to see if any of the rest of you have glossaries in some of your books.

"If one of your books has a glossary, you can give yourself a little pop quiz when you've finished reading the book. You can run your finger down the list of words in the glossary, stopping at each word to ask yourself, 'Does the definition that is in the book match what I know about the word? Does it add to what I know?' You can also think, 'Can I use this word to talk and teach others about my topic?' If you aren't sure that you really own that word, if you find yourself saying, 'Wait—what have I learned about that word?' then you can reread and learn the lingo for real!"

Knowing Ways Authors Use Features to Highlight Keywords, and Helping Authors Out When Necessary

Rally readers to join you in listing the text features authors often use to define keywords.

"Readers, can you come to the meeting area?" Once children had settled, I held a nonfiction book that contained lots of vocabulary-related text features, and said, "So let's do an inquiry where we list all the text features that authors include in books to help readers learn keywords. Call out one feature, and we'll see if this book has that feature."

The children called out "Glossary," and we found one in the book I held. I gestured to a word, written in bold, and they named that, and in a similar way, they pointed out that some books define keywords in text boxes. We found an index, and I explained, "An index tells the topics that the book addresses and the page numbers where you can find that information."

Then I said, "As you read, you may find even more ways that authors whisper in your ears to make sure that you know what a key word means. Text features don't just make a book *look* good; they help readers talk the talk and learn the lingo of their topics."

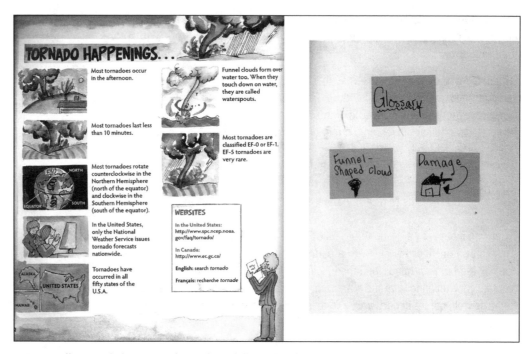

FIG. 7–1   Illustrated glossary with words and illustrations added by student

Point out that some books contain no text features to help with keywords, and suggest that in those instances, readers are called to do more.

"Many of your books will have these features to help you out, *but*," and I paused and leaned in, "sometimes, you may find that your book uses lots of keywords, but the author doesn't use any text features to spotlight them. When that happens, it's okay! Take a deep breath and remember this: the keywords are still there. You still need to learn them and use them to talk the talk of your topic. But now, *you* have to do the work that authors often do for their readers.

"*You* need to read closely and to pick keywords that are especially important. And if you want to help readers who will read the book after you, you can add text features that will help those readers.

"Look what Zach has done to help other readers understand the body parts of a whale." I held up Zach's diagram. It showed a photo of a whale. Zach labeled it with "Blowhole" and "Nostril," each with an arrow pointing to the body part.

"And look at what Aubrey did to make his own glossary at the back of *Tornados*." I showed them Aubrey's work.

"So, readers, will you and your partner see if there is a book in one of your baggies where the author hasn't given readers any help with keywords, and right now, while you are sitting here, will you start adding some help into that book?" Soon children had added work like that shown in Figure 7–2.

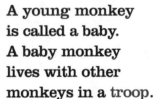

FIG. 7–2 Zach's topic vocabulary

Using Context to Build Knowledge of Unknown Words

IN THIS SESSION, you'll teach children to understand unde-fined keywords by using the *whole* page to figure out what those words mean.

GETTING READY

✔ Display the anchor chart "Talk the Talk! Read to Learn the Lingo!" (see Connection). 👆

✔ Prepare the demonstration text by masking some keywords. We highlighted the words *full-grown* and *distances*, starting on page 20 in *Tigers*, by Laura Marsh (see Teaching).

✔ Prepare to add two new strategy Post-its—"Use the WHOLE page to figure out what new keywords mean." and "Ask, 'What's it like or similar to?'"—to the anchor chart (see Link and Mid-Workshop Teaching). 👆

✔ Advise students to select a text containing keywords that they were confused by (see Share).

MINILESSON

CONNECTION

Talk to readers about your experiences learning a new language (Spanish), pointing out that it was hard to go beyond learning just a few common words.

"Readers, I remember that when I first started learning Spanish there were some things I learned quickly—like saying *hola*. That's *hello* in Spanish. And it was easy for me to learn to say *good-bye*, too. Do you know how to say *good-bye* in Spanish?" Some children called out *adios*. "Those words were easy for me, and some others were, too. But really learning Spanish so I could speak it and think it—that is taking me a lot of time. Learning a new language is nothing to sneeze at."

Point out that what the kids are doing is no less than learning a new language (e.g., tiger talk), that it is no surprise that this is hard, and that sometimes they'll confront words they just don't know.

"I'm telling you this because each one of you is, in a way, learning a new language every time you study up on a new topic. We are all learning tiger talk, and Thomas, are you learning weather talk? Are you starting to talk weather lingo?" He nodded vigorously and sat up a bit more. "You've all been working so hard to read it with me," I said, and tapped the heading of the chart.

> **ANCHOR CHART**
>
> Talk the Talk! Read to Learn the Lingo!
>
> • Expect and look out for keywords.
> • Look for and use features to help.

"But even after you get ready to read by looking out for keywords and using features to find them in your books, sometimes you still can't figure out what a key word means. It's locked! You can't get in and *understand* the word. But do you give up and just skip it? Oh, no, not you! No siree! Readers don't give up. Readers find the keys to unlock keywords in their books." I held an imaginary key in my hand and turned my wrist as if opening a lock.

❖ **Name the teaching point.**

"Today I want to teach you that when readers run into a keyword, they work hard to unlock it. They use the *whole* page and everything they know about the topic to figure out what it probably means."

TEACHING

Demonstrate how you unlock difficult keywords by drawing on the whole page and the text features when reading a sentence from the demonstration text. Try to keep kids participating in the work.

I turned to page 20 of *Tigers* and put it under the document camera. "Let's try this in *Tigers*. Read with me."

Tiger Talents

Tigers are full-grown when they leave their families.

I stopped and said, "This word here—*full-grown*—you all know the words *full* (like a full glass of water) and *grown* (like how big you have gotten). But the word *full-grown*? You probably have some general feeling that you know what it means, but are you sure you really own that word yet? Let's work with it. You need to make sure you truly know what it means so you can be sure you are grasping what this part of the book is teaching you."

"Let's get started. Is there a feature on the page that can help you unlock this keyword and really understand *full-grown*? No! So, we are going to need to use the *whole* page to help us figure this out!

"Are you ready to work hard and use the *whole* page?" I pushed up my sleeves and said, "Help me along."

Tigers are full-grown when they leave their families. They are big, heavy cats, but they can climb trees and jump great distances.

"Let's read *around* the keyword." I reread. "Hmm, . . . are you thinking that this word—*full-grown*—is describing what the tigers are like when they leave their families?" The children nodded. "So what are they like? It says they are big and heavy." I pointed to the pictures before thinking out loud, "I'm thinking that young tigers, smaller ones, don't leave. They stay until they are grown—*full-*grown—as big as they are going to get."

Vocabulary experts suggest that students work first on words that they "use but confuse."

Regardless of the text you choose to model, you'll want to choose vocabulary that is Tier II, and emphasize all that is gained by slowing down and working with words that you sort of know, but need to put into the context of the book.

Debrief, naming what you and the class have done that can be replicated with other pages, with other books, on other days.

"Notice that we sort of knew *full-grown*, but we didn't just say, 'Oh, that's good enough.' Instead, we worked to unlock it to really understand what the word means. To unlock it, we used the sentence around the keyword to help us. We also looked at the photograph." I held up two fingers to collect the strategies. "We also used parts of the word to help, like *full* and *grown*. Wow, that's three strategies to unlock this word. That's a lot of keys. Put those keys on your key chain. I bet you'll need those strategies to help you unlock keywords in your books." The children acted as if they were fastening keys to imaginary key chains. "All of this is work you can do anytime you read anything."

ACTIVE ENGAGEMENT

Give kids time to work together on determining the meaning of an unknown word.

"Don't put those keys away just yet. I'm wondering if you and your partner can figure out this keyword, too. I pointed to the word *distances*. "What is that word teaching us about tigers? You'll need use the *whole* page—the words *and* the pictures—to think about what this keyword might mean. First, let's read it."

> They are big, heavy cats, but they can climb trees and jump great distances. In fact, tigers can leap as
> far as 30 feet. That's as long as five adult men lying head to toe!

"Is there a part of this word, *distances*, that might help?" The class fell silent. "Hmm, . . . it looks like that key won't fit in the lock. Can you use the pictures?" The class nodded. "Try that key! And don't forget to use the words around the whole sentence. Reread the words around the keyword. See if that key unlocks it. What might this word mean? Turn and talk it out with your partner!"

LINK

Recap the strategies readers can use to understand unfamiliar vocabulary, cautioning children that these tips won't work for every word and that they need to use everything they know (every key they have) to unlock the keyword.

"Readers expect to find keywords in their books. The important work is to unlock them and really understand what they mean. That way, readers learn even more about their topics. So if you come across a keyword as you read, be sure to stop and get to work. You can take out your key chain and think about what strategies you know that might help. You

Research shows that being explicit in showing English language learners how to use context clues and pictures supports their vocabulary development. They will also benefit from direct instruction and demonstrations on how to look for and use cognates as they read text.

can use the *whole* page—the pictures and the words. You can even use parts of the word to help you." I paused to add the new strategy to the anchor chart. "Remember, though, not every key fits, so you'll want to practice using everything you know. Ready to get started? Off you go!"

ANCHOR CHART

Talk the Talk! Read to Learn the Lingo!

- Expect and look out for keywords.
- Look for and use features to help.
- **Use the WHOLE page to figure out what new keywords mean.**

Use the WHOLE page to figure out what new keywords mean

Coaching Students to Use Meaning, Structure/Syntax, and Visual Cues

Decide which students to pull for a series of guided reading sessions.

You'll support readers today as usual, with a combination of conferring and small-group work. For about ten minutes of today's workshop, you may decide to pull together a guided reading group to support kids who are below benchmark and need support solving words using an orchestration of meaning, structure/syntax, and visual cues (MSV). By supporting youngsters with books that have been well introduced, you can help readers move into the next reading levels. Of course, guided reading is not the only vehicle for supporting a youngster with a new book that is just a bit of a stretch (you can also do this with shared reading or with a good conference), but guided reading is one good way to go.

Start the guided reading with a book introduction.

In your guided reading group, you can decide whether the book introduction needs to support all three areas (MSV) or whether this group of kids especially needs support in one or two of those dimensions of reading. If you decide to give a book introduction in which you support all three areas, remember that you do not need to give this support to *all* parts of the book. Your goal is not to eliminate difficulty but to give just enough support so that students can put their strategies to work when they are having difficulty.

Your book intro may sound like this: "This book is called *Bird Beaks*. In this book, you are going to learn all about the beaks that birds have. You are going to learn what they look like and the shapes, as well as the uses that birds have for their beaks. Do you know some things already, even just by looking at the cover? Okay, look at this bird and its beak together. This beak looks like it is a bit curvy. Maybe that helps it hold or catch the fish that is in the mouth.

"Do you also see how there is a word off to the side? *Wren*. That is what this bird, here in the picture, is called. Each page has a different label that you can try to read the best you can. Do you see this bird? Do you know what it is? Look for the label and break

up the word. *Spoonbill*. Yes, that is what type of bird this is! I like the name because the beak looks like a spoon. At the end of the book, try to say *all* the things that you learn about how the beaks look different and what the birds do with them. Are you ready? Let's read."

Coach readers during the guided reading, using lean prompts and directions. Then give readers an explicit teaching point at the end.

You will want to prompt readers to use MSV as they are word solving. When you hear a student make an error using phonics, say to the reader, "Did that make sense? Go back, reread, and think about what would make sense." Sometimes a student might say a word that actually makes sense but is not the right word. Say to the student, "Does that look right? Reread and say the first part of the word, thinking about what would make sense." Giving these types of prompts to help cross-check their reading will help students develop an inner ear for the way they should be talking to themselves as they read in their mind.

If you give students a couple of prompts and they are still unable to solve the word, don't let them grow frustrated. Say to them, "Could it be . . . ," and then fill in the word that it is. If the student nods his head yes or shakes his head no, prompt the student to reread by saying, "Go back and check to see that the word looks right and makes sense."

You may find with many readers that you want to prompt for more fluency work, either scooping up more words to preserve the syntax or reading with more expression in their voice. Prompt students to reread with more fluency by saying something like "Does that sound right? Go back and smooth this part out."

After the students have read the book (or part of the book) and talked about what the book taught them, give them an explicit teaching point to practice on a reread or think about as they finish the text.

"Readers, let me give you another tip to help you read and understand those tricky keywords in your books. When you've said the word as best you can and you've used the whole page to help you, but it still isn't crystal clear what the word means, you can ask questions. One question that helps is this: 'What sort of thing might this word be like or similar to?' Like on this page of storms, Stella read these sentences:

> *When it roars past, it can knock down fences. In Australia, they call the storms willy-willys.*

"Stella thought, 'Willy-willys?' That's not *hard* to read, but I don't get what it means.' So Stella asked herself some questions. She asked, 'What sort of thing might this word be like or similar to? It won't be *exactly* the same, but close.'

"Stella reread and noticed the book said that during willy-willys, the wind blows sand across the land. She stopped to think, 'What sort of thing might be close to this?' and she thought, 'Oh, it's some sort of a storm. It's sort of like a dust storm or a rainstorm but with sand!'

"As you continue reading, and you come across new keywords, use the *whole* page to help you. Ask yourself questions like 'What do I know that is like this? What *might* it be similar to?' This might help you in understanding those keywords. I'll add this strategy to our chart."

ANCHOR CHART

Talk the Talk! Read to Learn the Lingo!

- Expect and look out for keywords.
- Look for and use features to help.
- Use the WHOLE page to figure out what new keywords mean.
- **Ask, "What's it like or similar to?"**

Ask, "What's it like or similar to?"

Teaming Up with Partners to Build Keywords Together

Rally readers to work together to talk about what an unknown word might mean.

"Readers, have you ever heard the saying 'Two heads are better than one'? To figure something out, sometimes it is easier to work with another person. Some of you have words that you still *really* haven't figured out yet or ones that you *think* you know. Bring those to your partner and see if both of you can figure them out or check them together. Have a little talk to build a definition that makes sense. Use the chart to help you. Partner 1 can go first, and then, Partner 2, you can share."

I circulated among the readers, prompting them to reread, to use the things on the anchor chart, raise questions, and respond to their partners. I prompted readers by saying things such as "Readers, it helps to reread as you are talking about what words mean," or "Readers, remember, help your partner try one or two things on the chart to really understand what the new words mean," or "Make sure you understand what your partner is saying. Ask, 'What do you mean? Can you give me an example?'"

FIG. 8–1   Some students use individual Figure It Out cards to scaffold questioning and talk together.

Solving Words Takes Strategic and Flexible Thinking

IN THIS SESSION, you'll demonstrate how figuring out keywords requires both persistence and practice.

CONNECTION

Remind students that they have learned to use everything they know to unlock the meaning of a key word.

"Yesterday, you learned that if you are reading along and everything is going smoothly and then—whoa—you get stuck on a word, you have keys to try unlocking it. You learned that you can roll up your sleeves and get to work. You can use the whole page and think about everything you know about the topic to unlock those keywords. Sometimes, though, all it takes is figuring out how to *say* the word because sometimes that tough word is one you already know."

❖ **Name the teaching point.**

"Today I want to teach you that when readers are stuck on a key word, they know to *play around* with the word, like you might play around with a key in the lock, trying it one way and then another, and sometimes—presto!—they find the way to unlock it."

TEACHING

Model how to play with a word to figure it out, noting that sometimes the word may be a familiar one.

"You are second-graders—you know a *lot* about word solving—and the truth is, if you think of different strategies you know for solving words, more likely than not, you'll be able to figure words out, even when they are super-duper tricky. Then you can add even more words to your word list. They won't always be words that are keywords and part of the lingo of the topic, but they will be words that *you* figured out on your own! So let's play with some super tricky words." Some kids giggled, but I kept on. I opened to page 12, where the word *territory* was emphasized with highlighter tape.

GETTING READY

✔ Prepare your demonstration text by highlighting words with which to practice today's strategy. We focus on *territory*, *carnivores*, *hooved*, and *buffalo* on pages 10 and 12 of *Tigers*, by Laura Marsh (see Teaching and Active Engagement).

✔ Locate a word with a pronunciation guide. We use *Siberian* from page 25 of *Tigers* (see Mid-Workshop Teaching).

✔ Ask children to bring a text with hard-to-solve keywords to practice rereading in a smooth voice (see Share).

✔ Display the "Talk the Talk! Read to Learn the Lingo!" chart on the easel for readers to refer to (see Share).

"Let's read this page together."

Tiger Turf

Besides hunting, tigers spend a lot of time marking their territory.

When I got to the highlighted word, I stopped. "Yikes, what is this? Don't tell me if you know. Play with the word in your head. I will play with the word out loud. I am going to try to say it a couple different ways, using what I know about how words and parts of words work together, and see if I can figure out what the word is. Maybe it's a word I already know!

"Okay, I see the whole word. I am going to say it in parts and then put the parts together." I read each chunk with long vowel sounds and then pronounced the whole word: /tee-rite-oh-ree/. I looked up, confused. "Let me keep playing and try it another way, this time with short vowel sounds, "/Teh-rit-ory/. Territory! Oh, yes, I've heard that word before. Is that what you came up with in your head? Territory? It's talking about an area that an animal protects from other animals. The tigers are marking the part of the land where they live."

Debrief and name the process you just went through so that students can replicate it later with another text.

I debriefed my process to help students transfer the strategy to their own reading. "Did you see how I'm trying lots of strategies? I'm being strategic, playing around with the word until I get it. Now I can add it to my lingo to talk the talk of this book."

ACTIVE ENGAGEMENT

Provide the chance to practice playing with words in a different part of the text.

"Now try a couple of difficult words with your partner." I turned to page 10, where I'd highlighted several words: *carnivores*, *hooved*, and *buffalo*. I placed the page under the document camera as I voiced over directions. "Work together with your partner to unlock these words. Use all of your keys! Remember, play with the word to say it a few different ways. Use different sounds and chunk it different ways. When you have figured out *all three words*, put your thumb on your knee so that I know you are ready!"

LINK

Restate the importance of being strategic and flexible word solvers, and remind readers how this will help them speak the language of a topic.

"Remember, if you get to a word that feels tough or looks strange, another way you can unlock that word is by playing with it—saying it a few different ways, using what you know about how parts of words work together, because sometimes, when you figure out how to *say* a word, you realize you've heard that word before and already know what it means. Then you'll have even more lingo to talk the talk like real experts!"

You'll notice that, once again, we are using Tigers from our shared-reading session. We've purposely chosen a page that the students haven't read together for this minilesson so that the word-solving practice is authentic and flexible.

Be mindful that some of your English language learners will still need visuals and graphic depictions of concepts and words to assist them with this task.

Coaching Students to Think as They Read

Pull a small group of readers who are working above the grade level benchmark and are ready to move up a text level.

As you confer with readers and pull small groups today, you may decide to work for a few minutes with students who are ready to move up to, for example, a level N or O text. With these students, you may decide to do a book introduction that leans heavily on how the text is organized and a couple of key concepts that they will learn about in this text. You may draw their attention to one or two key vocabulary words. Show students how the text will support their understanding of keywords. Texts at level N and beyond often do not have a feature to spotlight keywords, but the words are usually defined on the page, often in the context surrounding the word. These texts sometimes contain glossaries that help readers learn more about the keywords and their meanings.

Then give kids the text to read. Your role will not be to support them in the actual reading of the text, but instead will be to prompt them in lean ways, as a coach would coach a player during a game, on how to think in various parts of the text. You might prompt students by saying things like "Think about how this information fits with what you just read," or "What does that mean? Use the picture and the text features on the page," or "Can you think about another example of what this part is talking about?" or "Go back and reread that part thinking about what it is teaching you."

Conduct a small-group strategy lesson for readers who need support in word solving.

Another choice for this portion of the reading workshop is to pull a small group of readers who especially need support in chunking words and being more efficient in their word solving. You may decide to work on "crashing" the parts of a word together and then thinking about whether the resulting word makes sense in the sentence.

You may start by saying, "We are going to work on reading longer words. Reading one part and then putting it together with the next part and so on is called crashing the

---

MID-WORKSHOP TEACHING
Pronouncing Words Is a Process

"Readers, sometimes when we get to a tricky keyword, we have to play with it a bit, trying it one way and another before we figure out what the word means and how to say it. Other times, guess what? Sometimes, there is a *feature* that authors give us to help us say the word exactly the right way! When that happens, it's like hitting a jackpot! The feature can help us know exactly how to pronounce the word.

"Pronunciation is the way we say words, and pronouncing new words can be tough. *Sometimes* authors include a pronunciation key to help out! Like in our shared reading book, *Tigers*." I opened to page 25, put the book under the document camera and pointed to the word *Siberian*.

"Laura Marsh knew that this word might be difficult to pronounce even if we played around with it and did all we could to say the word, so she put, in parentheses, the letters that make the sounds for each part! You'll notice some letters are capitalized, too. That's so when we say that part, we say it a little stronger than the rest. Try pronouncing the word with me!" I tapped the parts of the word as I read them, and then put the parts together to read the word *Siberian*.

(si-BEER-ee-uhn) Siberian

"If you see this nifty little feature, called the pronunciation key, in your book, use it! It's there to help you read your best *and* talk the talk of your book! This tool isn't always there to help, but when it is—hooray! You hit the jackpot. You can use the pronunciation key to say the word just right and then make sure you know what the word means. Back to it!"

---

word. You might have practiced this in first grade. In any case, let's practice it together, so that when you encounter longer words, you have another strategy to try."

Choose a word like *endangered*. Write the first part of a word (*en*) on a white board and have the students read it. Then write the next part (*dang*) and have them read the two parts together. Then write the third part (*er*) and read from the start of the word, /endanger/. Finally write the last part of the word and have the students read the whole word, *endangered*. Then show the students a sentence strip with the word used in context and have them read it to see if it makes sense. Remind them that they may have to try saying the word a few different ways before it makes sense to them. Repeat this with a couple of words and then have readers read their own books. As they come across long words, coach readers to crash the parts together and make certain that the word they've read makes sense.

Knowing and Fixing Problems Independently

Explain to readers the importance of taking ownership of monitoring reading.

"Readers, find a place in one of your books where you used some keys to unlock a keyword." I gave students a moment to select a book and then continued, "It is a really big deal that you're the type of readers who know and fix your own problems.

"You aren't just unlocking keywords. You are unlocking the key to *reading*. You've discovered that you don't wait around for me or for someone else to remind you what to do. *You* are the key to your own reading. You've worked hard to use different strategies, you use strategies together, you try one strategy and then another: you are strategic readers!"

I put my hand on my heart and gave a contented sigh. "This is too big of a moment to just skip over quickly. Take a moment to recall the strategies you've been using to unlock the keywords all by yourself and explain to your partner the work you've done. Don't just tell your partner the words; talk to your partner about the different keys you've been using—the *strategies*." I tapped the heading of the anchor chart. "Describe how you are becoming the key to your own reading, and make plans for what you'll continue to work on to unlock your reading life. Partner 1, you'll start the talk today. Get to it!"

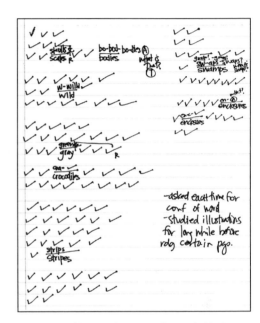

FIG. 9–1 This running record reveals that while the student is still making miscues as he reads, especially when he gets to domain-specific vocabulary, he is monitoring himself closely and consistently. This reading behavior is something all students should strive to develop.

ANCHOR CHART

Talk the Talk! Read to Learn the Lingo!

- Expect and look out for keywords.
- Look for and use features to help.
- Use the WHOLE page to figure out what new keywords mean.
- Ask, "What's it like or similar to?"

Rereading Like Experts

IN THIS SESSION, you'll show children the importance of rereading to grow more information about the topic.

GETTING READY

✔ Instruct children to bring book baggies to the meeting area and keep them hidden until the link (see Connection).

✔ Select a passage from your demonstration text to revisit and display. We've chosen to reread page 12 in *Tigers*, by Laura Marsh (see Teaching and Active Engagement).

✔ Display the anchor chart "Talk the Talk! Read to Learn the Lingo!" (see Teaching and Active Engagement and Share).

✔ Prepare to add a new strategy Post-it—"Reread it like an expert."—to the anchor chart (see Share).

✔ Make sure kids have a book ready to practice rereading like experts in their partnerships (see Share).

MINILESSON

CONNECTION

Tell a story that illustrates how stopping to unlock keywords can slow readers down. Then, connect this to the importance of rereading.

"Let me tell you a quick story about the day I moved into my apartment," I started as the students settled into the meeting area. "I parked the moving truck at the curb and started to unload my things. The front door was locked, so I had to set down my boxes and take out my key ring. The front door had *two* locks. I tried one key and then another, but neither worked." I acted this out as I told the story to the class, miming putting keys into locks, wiggling the doorknob, taking out and selecting another key from my pretend key ring. "I tried again and finally managed to unlock the door and go inside. 'I'm in at last!' I thought." Some of the kids gave a little victory sign as I pretended to pick the boxes back up and continued on with my story.

"I picked up my boxes, walked into the building and straight to my apartment door, and what do you know? *Another* locked door. This wasn't going very smoothly. So I got my keys out *again* and worked to unlock *that* door, too. Once I had all those doors unlocked, moving the rest of the boxes went so much more smoothly.

"This story reminds me of the work you're doing to unlock keywords in your books. There will be times you figure out keywords right away and other times when you have to work *especially* hard, trying a few strategies before you unlock the word. Unlocking word after word can slow you down at first, but once you unlock keywords, they are just like those doors to my apartment. They stay open. And when you reread you can move through information more smoothly to open the door to even more knowledge."

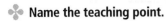 **Name the teaching point.**

"Today I want to teach you that once readers have unlocked keywords in their books, they know it helps to reread—this time moving more smoothly through the parts, scooping up the keywords to grow even more knowledge about the topic."

TEACHING AND ACTIVE ENGAGEMENT

Revisit a passage to demonstrate rereading to show understanding.

I put page 12 of *Tigers* under the document camera and said, "Yesterday we read this part and stopped to unlock—how do you say this word again?" I pointed to the word *territories*. "And what does it have to do with tigers?" I scratched my head and suggested, "Turn and remind each other. If you need to refresh your memory, call on everything you know about unlocking keywords!" I pointed to the "Talk the Talk! Read to Learn the Lingo!" anchor chart.

After a minute, I tapped the text box at the bottom of the page and continued, "Ah, yes! This word is *territories*. Magali remembered that a territory is an area that an animal protects from other animals. Who else remembered?" Heads nodded. "Porter remembered that tigers have their own territories and spend a lot of time marking them.

"Now that the word is unlocked, let's reread this part, moving through the information more smoothly this time around, scooping up the key word with the rest of the information to grow even more knowledge about the topic." I read alongside the class. Stopping at the end of the page I said, "That sounded *so* much smoother, and now I understand even more that this part taught us that tigers do *different* things to mark their territories so that other tigers stay away."

Channel partners to try this work on a different familiar page, first thinking about tricky words and then rereading the page smoothly to boost understanding.

Flipping back to page 10 I said, "There was another part yesterday where you stopped to unlock a few keywords." I tapped the words *carnivores*, *hooved*, and *buffalo*. "How do you say those words again? And how do they help us grow knowledge about tigers? Turn and remind each other. Go through each word to make sure you know. Once you've thought about how these words sound and what they mean, reread this part, but this time move more smoothly through the parts, scooping up the keywords to grow even more knowledge about tigers."

I moved among the partnerships, coaching readers first to monitor—to slow down and unlock keywords—and then to reread, scooping up even more words and smoothing out their reading voices. I coached, reacted to improved fluency, modeled when needed, and whispered lean prompts. "You unlocked it. Now reread and scoop those words," and "Try it again. A little bigger scoop." I nudged partners to listen to each other as I moved swiftly around the room. As readers moved through this process, I stopped to make sure they were not only reading the words, but also understanding their reading by asking, "So, what is the author teaching you about tigers in this part?"

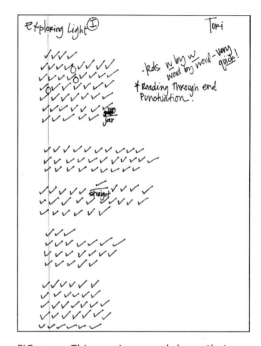

FIG. 10–1 This running record shows that while the reader has a high rate of accuracy, she does not attend to end punctuation. Additionally, you'll notice the teacher mentions the reader reads quickly, but word-by-word as she moves through the text.

LINK

Name the transferable work readers did, and coach them to practice in their own texts.

"I know you heard and felt how much smoother and clearer your reading became when you unlocked and then reread those keywords in *Tigers*. Once you unlocked the keywords, you reread, scooping up the keywords to grow even more knowledge about your topics.

"Take out one of your books and find a part where you had to stop to unlock some keywords. Remind yourself of how those words are *key* to growing knowledge about your topic and then reread the part you found them in, making sure to sound smoother, taking even bigger scoops of words, remembering to include that keyword right alongside the rest of the words!"

You'll want to consider having several tool cards made and ready to leave for students who need reminders of how to scoop words. Consider inviting students who need a reminder to pick one up before they head off to private reading time today.

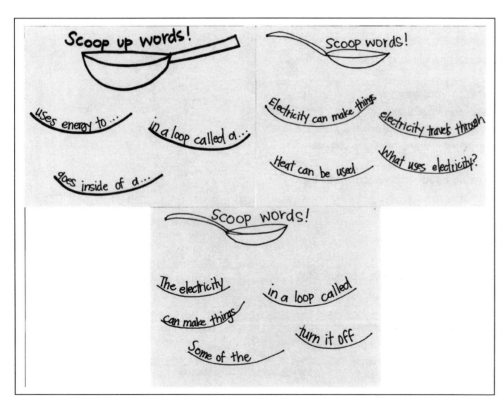

FIG. 10–2   A scoop card reminds students to put words into three-, four-, and five-word scoops to make reading smooth and more fluent.

Supporting Students in Unlocking Keywords and Rereading Like an Expert

Use the anchor chart to assess and teach readers.

As the second bend of your nonfiction unit is winding down, you'll want to take time to make sure that readers are not only using the strategies to talk the talk and learn the lingo of their topics but also that they are flexible and strategic in their learning. Pull up alongside a reader, with the anchor chart in mind, and listen in to check and see if children are doing the following:

◆ Looking for and using features to help understand key vocabulary

◆ Using the *whole* page to figure out what new keywords mean

◆ Rereading the text like an expert after they hit a bumpy spot

Take this opportunity to lead coaching conferences with individual readers or table conferences with small groups of readers. Instead of interrupting the reader and

---

MID-WORKSHOP TEACHING **Matching Voices with Information**

"Readers, your reading sounds smooth and like an expert. You're unlocking key-words, rereading, and scooping those words to read and understand your books," I said from the middle of the classroom. I waited a moment until all eyes were on me before continuing.

"Make sure that the voice you're reading with matches the information in the book. When you read surprising information, use a surprised voice. When the information you read makes you worry, you read with a tense voice to express that worry. You might even read information that makes you feel sad. Change your voice to show it. Think about what you just read and ask yourself, 'How does this part want to be read? How does this information make me feel? What does this information make me think?' Then reread with that feeling and thinking in your voice." I looked at the class to gauge for understanding and continued.

"Remember, you should know *why* you are changing your reading voice. If I asked you, 'Why are you making your voice sound that way?' you wouldn't shrug your shoulders and say, 'I don't know.'

"As you read and change your voice, make sure that you use the clues in your books to help you think about how it should go. For example you might read this page about hurricanes like this," and I began to read with a charged voice.

"If you asked me, 'Why did you read that way?' I would say to you, 'I read it that way because the author is telling us about danger here and how fast and strong the storm is. So I want to show how dangerous it is with my voice and make my voice strong and powerful like the hurricane the author is teaching me about.'

"Right here, right now, think about what you just read. Ask yourself, 'How does this part make me feel?' and reread it, making your voice match the information you're reading and thinking about. Share one part with the person sitting closest to you. Read it aloud and then tell why you read it the way you did. Tell how you were feeling and what you did to make your voice match the information you were reading. Have at it."

---

demonstrating, coach into the reading when you hear him get to a new vocabulary word. You may say, "Use the whole page. Figure out what the word means *before* you move on." Or, "Does that make more sense? You got it. Now go back and reread it like an expert."

You may find that the work you do to coach an individual reader can be turned into an opportunity to remind the entire table of readers to be strategic with their word solving. Stop the entire table of readers and offer strategies from the chart, such as "Readers, remember to use the *whole* page to figure out what a new keyword means, and once you've figured the word out, go back to reread like the expert you're becoming."

It's likely that you'll want students to do some self-reflection and goal-setting as you wind down the bend. Ask a student to reflect on the strategies on the chart and think about which strategies he is confident at using as a reader, and then teach the readers how to make plans to try the other strategies as well. Have the reader point to the strategies he is planning to continue to practice and improve upon as he continues his independent reading time.

Think, too, about the readers you see and hear doing "hit and miss" work as they read. It may be that you see readers show evidence of solving and understanding vocabulary but not show consistency in monitoring when they come to a word they do not know or understand. If you have students who are reading through words or, worse, omitting words completely and reading on, take time to remind and reteach that catching oneself as a reader is a *good* habit to have. The only person who can fix their reading and make sure it makes sense is the *reader*. Encourage and cheer on their bravery when they get to a word and pause to solve.

Practicing to Reread and Sound Like Experts

Announce that readers will perform parts for reading partners and give each other tips.

"Readers, to speak the language of a topic, you can practice by rereading parts like experts." I added the new strategy to the chart.

ANCHOR CHART

Talk the Talk! Read to Learn the Lingo!

- Expect and look out for keywords.
- Look for and use features to help.
- Use the WHOLE page to figure out what new keywords mean.
- Ask, "What's it like or similar to?"
- **Reread it like an expert.**

Reread it like an expert

Talk the Talk! Read to Learn the (Lingo!)

Expect and look out for keywords

Look for and use features to help

Use the WHOLE page to figure out what new keywords mean

Ask, "What's it like or similar to?"

Reread it like an expert

"We're going to practice performing our pages to our partners, rereading them like experts. Find a place in your book that you'd like to perform. If you aren't the partner that's rereading like an expert, you might give your partner tips to sound more like an expert by saying things like 'Make your voice match the information!' or 'Read in bigger scoops!' and 'Pay attention to the punctuation!'"

Talk the Talk and Walk the Walk! Using Lingo to Teach Others

MINILESSON

In the connection, you might recall the story of the time you felt confused listening to an expert talk the talk of a topic and give an example of how the way you sound can reveal what you know. You might say, "My nephew, Troy, found some skateboarding books for me to read so I could talk the skateboarding talk. So yesterday on the phone I said, 'Hey, Troy, the other day I was watching ESPN2 and I saw this skater do a rad trick. I was stoked. It was like an air run. I mean, an air board?' Then, Troy interrupted me, 'Auntie, the trick, the airwalk grab, is super hard. You need a niner just to pull it off. I could teach you how." I laughed after we hung up because I guess I've gotten good enough at talking the talk, at using the lingo, that he thinks I'm about to do airboard grabs myself! No way! I sure fooled him."

Then, explain that that's how it goes when you read about a topic. You might say, "You begin to talk like an expert, and pretty soon people treat you like an expert. Talking the talk is a big part of *really* reading about a topic, *really* developing some expertise on the topic."

Name the teaching point to your students. You might say, "Today I want to teach you that when readers read nonfiction, they don't only *read* keywords and *learn* information. They start to *use* keywords to think and talk about the topic. In that way, the reader begins to own the language of the text."

During the teaching, you might use *Tigers* to show students how to skim a section of the text, looking for keywords that help teach and tell what the part is mostly about. Encourage students to look with you as you put the pages up on the document camera. Quickly jot a couple of these words on Post-its and begin to talk to the class about what the part teaches about tigers. Use the keywords. Each time you use one, point to the Post-it. Ask students, "Did you notice that when I was telling you about this part, I used the keywords when I was talking? That helps me to *own* the talk of my topic!"

During the active engagement, project another part of the demonstration text. Ask students to quickly skim the page and find the keywords. Have a few kids name out the keywords in this section. Record them for kids to remember. Then ask them to turn and talk to partners, encouraging students to try to talk again, longer and stronger, using more keywords to teach each other about this part of the book.

When you give the link, you might say, "You've learned so much about talking the talk of your books. You aren't just the kind of readers who *talk the talk* of your books and topics. You are actually *walking the walk*. That means you are really knowledgeable about your topics and are really starting to *own* these words. It's one thing to *talk the talk*, but it's even bigger and better when you can *walk the walk*—when you can teach others all you've learned."

CONFERRING AND SMALL-GROUP WORK

Then you will want to confer and pull small groups of readers to work on several things. You might spend a few minutes working with a small group of students who would benefit from additional support in paying close attention to the keywords in their books. You may decide to set students up to work in partnerships. Consider placing Post-its on two pages of one partner's book. Write keywords from the text on Post-its for students to discuss and use as they finish a section or a book. Have students work as partners to both read and then discuss the book, using those keywords. You might also have the partnerships decide if they need to add keywords from their reading. As the partnerships continue, mark another spot with a Post-it and have students decide on keywords from the section that need to be added to the Post-it note. After repeated practice with one partner's book, have the partnerships do the same work, without your scaffolded Post-its, with the second partner's book. You may, at this point, leave the partners so that they continue working together, thinking and talking about keywords, independently. Then you will be able to confer with other students as the first partnership continues to work together.

Mid-Workshop Teaching

During the mid-workshop teaching, remind students that the mark of any expert is to be the kind of thinker who uses multiple strategies to figure out keywords. Remind students that their work as nonfiction readers is both to take in information, paying careful attention to and being on the lookout for keywords, and to carry those words forward and use them when they talk about their learning with others. Give readers a heads up that during today's share, they will practice owning keywords by using them to teach others about a part of their book.

SHARE

During the share, return to the important work of today's minilesson, giving kids extended time to talk about their learning. Combine partnerships into groups of four ("rug clubs") and let each member talk the talk and walk the walk with the group. Have students use their books and keywords to briefly teach a couple of the most important things that they learned. Remind the listeners that they have a job as well. You may say to them, "Remember, listeners, don't just take in information. Ask questions like 'Can you give an example?' or 'Why is that important?' or 'What do you mean? Can you say more about that?'" Remind students to use their books and show the parts that teach more about what they are sharing with their rug clubs. As the share closes, celebrate when kids confidently talk the talk, owning keywords and using lingo to sound like the experts they have become.

FIG. 11–1   Rug Club Game Mats help clubs practice listening and talking together. Students make game pieces and play their pieces to help each other talk long about their topic.

Growing Knowledge across Books! Getting Ready to Read (and Learn) a Bunch!

IN THIS SESSION, you'll teach readers how to set themselves up for reading not just one book on a topic but several.

GETTING READY

✔ Compile text sets of books rubber-banded together and put a few of these into each child's book baggie if you have enough or otherwise into a new partnership baggie (see Connection).

✔ Gift wrap a new demonstration text that connects (in some way) to the demonstration text you used across Bend II. Then, tie the two texts together with string. We use *Amazing Animals: Tigers*, by Valerie Bodden, because it is another tiger book at the same level of text complexity, offering information that echoes the first text while also offering opportunities to contrast details (see Connection).

✔ Create a new anchor chart titled "Experts Grow Knowledge Across Books" and be prepared to add the strategy "Notice parts that go together." (see Link).

✔ Write a Post-it note that includes an idea the demonstration text taught and something the reader wonders about that idea. Leave it in your demonstration text (see Mid-Workshop Teaching).

✔ Invite children to bring a set of books that go together to the meeting area (see Share).

MINILESSON

CONNECTION

Reveal that the book fairy has returned with a new gift of knowledge. Build suspense about its content before revealing that it is another text about tigers, thus setting readers up to understand the bend's purpose.

"Readers, before you come to the meeting area, look up here! The book fairy has done it again!" I held my discovery up high for all to see and speculate about. It was another gift-wrapped book and, what's more, it was bound together along with our well-worn copy of *Tigers*, by Laura Marsh.

"A new book!" someone proclaimed.

"Readers, another gift of knowledge? We must be the book fairy's favorite second-grade class! Let's not wait a second more! Let's open this book up. We've got some knowledge to grow!" I promptly removed the colorful paper to reveal the new text.

"Another tigers book! No wonder it was bound to our other tigers book! They're about the same topic! I've seriously been craving more information about tigers ever since we read this." I held up our familiar text. "Haven't you? We love tigers!"

Explain to children that in the upcoming bend, they'll all have opportunities to read text sets of books on different topics. Also share the news that you've already left them some text sets in their book baggies.

"Readers, we are starting a new bend in our unit. For the next while, you're going to be able to read not just *one* book on a topic, but a bunch. You see, when you get started reading information books, it is a bit like when you get started eating potato chips. You can't eat just one! You read one book about trains, and then you get so excited about trains that you just *need* to read more about them.

"Having a class book fairy has been so nice that I decided that every one of you deserves your own book fairy. So I pretended to be a book fairy and I delivered some new materials into your book baggies. In your baggie, you'll find a few books rubber-banded together on the *same* topic. So, today, you will be looking for not just single books on single topics to read, but a group of books on a topic.

"For the minilesson today, will you choose one text set of books (that will be two or three books on one topic) and bring that over to our meeting area? Let's get ready for workshop!"

❖ **Name the teaching point.**

"Today I want to teach you that when readers read a bunch of books on one topic, they get themselves ready not just by looking over *one* book but by looking over all the books. Readers especially think about how all their books on a topic seem to go together."

TEACHING AND ACTIVE ENGAGEMENT

Channel children to investigate their sets of books on a topic, thinking about how the new books go together.

"So, to start your study of a topic, you'll want to spread your books out in front of you to take a sneak peek not just of one book but of your *topic*. Think especially about how the different books on a topic go together. You already know they will all be about a topic—like bugs—but when you look *inside* the books and *inside* the topic, how do the books go together?"

The students took off the rubber bands that bound their books together and began noticing similar chapters and key-words and photographs across the different books on a topic. I interjected, "Some of you are noticing that the tables of contents in the different books suggest that some of the same chapters have the same information. Keep skimming and thinking, 'How do these books go together?'"

I coached a couple of students in the back row to move to the back of their books to read and compare the glossary pages, and they immediately noticed overlapping vocabulary. I announced to the entire class, "These readers are finding that some keywords in the glossaries are the same across the two books! Look to see if your books use overlapping vocabulary, too!"

Rally partnerships to share observations about how books in their text sets go together.

I got everyone's attention, "Remember! You are not just sneak-peeking one book, but you are sneak-peeking a topic. Can you share with your partner what you found out about how your books go together? I'll give you a minute to share."

We recommend that you lavishly wrap the set of books, with bows and ribbons, to make this especially celebratory. Play up the idea that a real book fairy left this gift.

The children will choose either a text set from their own baggies, if you have books enough to put two or three text sets in each child's baggie, or from a partnership baggie. Individuals need their own text set. You could, alternatively, tweak the minilesson and channel kids to shop for one set of books—their first topic.

FIG. 12–1   A new demonstration text is wrapped and bound to the one from Bend II.

Students began sharing with their partners as I did a quick lap around the meeting area, listening in to make certain students were talking across the texts. Many students noticed parts of books that had similar photographs or illustrations. Others talked about how the books had chapters with similar names.

I voiced over to the class, "Elijah found that his books go together in an unusual way. His topic is soccer. One book is on kids' soccer teams and one is on pro soccer. He decided that first a kid plays on a kid team and then he grows up to play pro, so he thinks the kids' soccer book comes first. I heard Leslie say she has books on different kinds of dance. She knows the most about ballet, so she is going to read that one first."

Debrief in a way that names the work that is transferable to other topics and other days.

"Readers, I hope you are noticing that when you get ready to read a bunch of books on a topic, it helps to look over not just one book but the collection of books. As you do that, you can think about how the books are similar and different, and sometimes you can start making plans for which book you will read first and which one will come next."

LINK

Introduce the new chart that will accumulate the third bend's teaching.

"Getting yourself ready to read a *topic* means that you can sneak-peek a few books at a time! You just got yourselves ready to grow knowledge about one topic, and when you're ready, you can do this with the other topics in your baggie as well. You can look to see which sections and chapters will be the same, which keywords might be the same, or you can even think about whether there is one book that you should read first! Let's start a chart to help us keep track of what we need to do to become topic experts."

"Remember, as you finish your first topic and you need more books, choose another group of books from your baggies. By the end of workshop today, you all should refill your baggies with new books and topics for the week! Okay, off you go to read and study your books!"

FIG. 12–2 Two boys sneak peek their topic set to discover similar keywords in the glossary.

As you enter into this new bend, you'll want to be sure children are carrying the strategies they learned from the first part of the unit. You'll notice that the language of "growing knowledge" is kept consistent to offer students repeated practice with the skills and strategies they've already learned as they move through Bend III.

Experts Grow Knowledge across Books!

Notice parts that go together

ANCHOR CHART

Experts Grow Knowledge across Books

- **Notice parts that go together.**

Studying Reading Logs and Conferring Notes to Gain a Wealth of Information

Get the new work going in the beginning of this new bend.

The launch of a new bend is a perfect time to take stock of what readers have been doing both inside and outside of workshop. You may decide to make today a day full of one-on-one conferences, checking in not only on reading behaviors and thinking but also on students' reading logs and behaviors outside of class. You may start by saying to the whole class, "Readers, make sure your logs are out today. I want to study and admire your reading lives." Then, as you pull up to readers, consider talking about their reading patterns. Check reading logs to see how the volume, the number of pages read, is transferring between home and school. Do you see consistency, or are the

---

MID-WORKSHOP TEACHING   Using Post-it Notes to Capture Ideas and What the Reader Wonders

"Readers, eyes up for a quick minute." I stood next to the document camera, with my *Tigers* book held high in the air. "Albert Einstein, one of the smartest people in history, said, 'I have no special talent. I am only passionately curious.' I'm hoping each and every one of you is passionately curious, too! And that means that as you read, you'll wonder.

"I sometimes wonder about things myself," I said and showed students the Post-it I'd written about our shared book (see Figure 12–1).

I said, "You see how I learned a big idea, and then that got me wondering. I hope the same thing happens to you as you read." I showed the children that I marked the passage I read that made me think that thought, and pointed out, "Because I have marked the place where I got this idea, I can share it with my partner. I can also come back to this place and reread it if I learn more about this big idea. You ready to do this work? Off you go!"

FIG. 12–3   A Post-it showing my wondering

---

numbers way off? Do you notice a child is reading far fewer pages in class than out of class? You might say, "What is it that helps you read almost twice as many pages at home as at school?" Then point out examples of your observations. You could teach readers how to pace themselves, setting a goal of pages to get to before workshop ends.

Studying student reading logs can offer a wealth of information. You might study for the lens of rereading. Ask the reader to retell or summarize a book that you see he's reread a time or two. If a child has read a book, expect the summary to be comprehensive. As the reader summarizes, you will want to listen for both main topics and several details that go with each main topic. You may find the information progression especially helpful to have during this work. Use it as you listen in on student summaries and make plans for the next steps to lift the level of the students' summarizing.

Add a new type of small group: shared reading.

As you study your conferring notes, check to see if there is a group of students who may benefit from extending their time together as part of a shared reading group.

Offer these below-benchmark readers a double dip of shared reading starting today and meeting again over the next couple of days. You might decide to use a new text to do this work in place of the *Tigers* text you've been using during whole-class shared reading. Consider a companion text, perhaps a National Geographic book that teaches about another topic, such as sharks or planets. Any text that meets the group at their *instructional* level of text will work.

Pull the small group together and work through a text: predicting, confirming, word solving, and smoothing out reading voices. You may mark a spot or section that you'll read together and save the rest of the text for future meetings with the group. You might decide to divide the text into sections and do a bit of performance reading during the shared reading session. Consider having the small group divide into teams of two, tracking and following along as you mark the text for one partnership to read the captions while another reads the text and a third reads the other features (for example, the jokes along the edge, the text boxes, or the chapter headings). Consider marking the spots with a different color of Post-it flag for each partnership. After a day or two of practice and talking about the text, let the small group read to the rest of the class while their peers celebrate their reading.

DATE	HOME OR SCHOOL?	TITLE	PAGES	MINUTES	RATE IT!	REREAD IT!
3/17	S	Shark Attack	9	25		
3/17	H	Shark Attack	16	25		
3/18	S	Shark Attack	8	30	★★★ ★★	✓
3/18	H	Chomp!	18	25		
3/19	S	Chomp!	7	22	★★★	
3/19	H	Sharks	17	30		
3/20	S	Sharks	7	28		
3/20	H	Sharks	16	35		✓
3/21	S	Ocean life	8	26		
3/21	H	Ocean life	14	30	★★	

FIG. 12–4   Study logs to collect data about reading pace and volume

Magali's retell:

I learned that penguins have flippers. They eat fish. Their beaks are really sharp. Did you know other animals eat penguins? Like whales. Penguins dance. The dad takes care of the egg while the mom leaves to get food.

FIG. 12–5   Quickly capturing a student's retell allows you to determine next steps to lift the level of the student's summarizing.

Sharing New Knowledge

Get readers bragging about their new learning. Channel one partner to give the other a tour of the topic, sounding like an expert.

"Readers, bring a couple of the books that are on the topic you studied today and sit quickly beside your partner.

"Partner 2, will you go first? Will you give Partner 1 a tour of your study? Show what you did today, what you realized, and what you wondered. Make sure you sound like an expert and get your partner interested in your topic! The good news is that when you finish reading all there is to read on the topic, you'll be able to swap books.

"And listeners, will you make sure you really understand what your partner says about the books? Make sure what your partner says makes sense. If it doesn't, ask your partner to say more or to explain things a different way.

"Hopefully there will be time for you each to give the other a tour of your books—and of your topic."

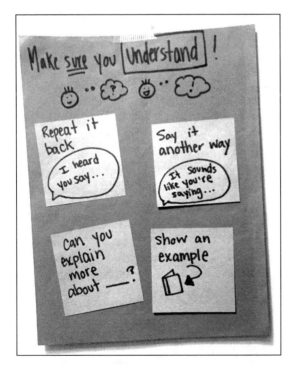

FIG. 12–6   Provide prompts to support partnerships in staying cognitively engaged in their book talks.

FIG. 12–7   Readers can jot ideas and questions on Post-its to ground their conversations.

Nonfiction Readers Add Information across Books

IN THIS SESSION, you'll teach readers that when you read about a topic, you try to add information together to learn about a sub-topic and the whole topic.

GETTING READY

✔ Display the anchor chart "Experts Grow Knowledge Across Books!" and have the strategy—"Add to what you know." ready to add to the chart (see Connection and Link).

✔ Select passages from two demonstration texts that support the skill of comparing and adding information. We're going to use *Tigers*, by Laura Marsh, and *Amazing Animals: Tigers*, by Valerie Bodden (see Teaching and Active Engagement).

✔ Check to be sure readers have Post-its to mark their books (see Link).

✔ Make sure readers have access to their book baggies (see Share).

MINILESSON

CONNECTION

Ask readers to reflect on the books they've read so far, and prompt them to ponder if any information was similar in different books.

"Readers, yesterday you began learning *a lot* about topics *across* your books. Nonfiction books really *are* like potato chips! They are so delicious, you can't read just one! Who here finished one book and thought, 'Yum! That knowledge was delicious! I must have another!'?" I rubbed my stomach as though I'd just consumed an actual meal. "It is impossible to have *just* one! Some of you read a couple of books about pets, some of you read a few books about different types of transportation, and some of you read several books about places in the world.

"Now, maybe there's such a thing as *too* many potato chips, but too many nonfiction books? Impossible! That's because when you read lots of books on a topic, your knowledge grows in epic ways until suddenly, you're the expert!" I touched the heading of the chart and looked out at each reader, meeting their eyes.

"You are *all* well on your way to becoming experts." My finger moved to the first bullet, and I continued, "Yesterday, even before you started reading one of the books, you skimmed and scanned the books on your topic, noticing things that went together across the books. You didn't just say, 'These two books are about weather.' You looked at the insides of the books and noticed that the two weather books *both* had parts about hurricanes. Cool, right? And *both* had parts about weather maps.

"Now that you've started to grow knowledge across books, I have a question for you. Really think about this before you answer it. Here is my question: When you started to read about your topics yesterday, reading book after book, did you read anything that was the same in a *few* of your books?"

ANCHOR CHART

Experts Grow Knowledge across Books!
• Notice parts that go together.

"Show me with thumbs on your knees." I looked around the room to check in on what students were thinking. I saw as many thumbs up as down and lots of in-between, noncommittal thumbs, so I said, "Some of you don't think so. Some of you aren't sure. A few of you think you did. Very in-ter-est-ing. I was hoping for unanimous thumbs on knees, but I see there is still work to be done!"

❖ **Name the teaching point.**

"Today I want to teach you that when readers have a couple books on *one* topic, they read a page in the second book on the topic and stop and think, 'Ohhhhhh! That adds on to what I already knew.' They know that the information from a page in one book can get added on to the information from a page of another book."

TEACHING AND ACTIVE ENGAGEMENT

Practice adding new information to prior knowledge by reading within a familiar text set.

"Let's try this with a topic we've already grown a lot of knowledge about." I revealed our new text about tigers. Reading the title page I said, "*Amazing Animals: Tigers*, by Valerie Bodden. As we read this book, be on the look-out for information that is the same as in *Tigers,* by Laura Marsh, and for information that adds on.

"If you see something that makes you go, 'Ohh! That adds on to what I already know!' will you put your thumb up? Then we will stop and talk about how the information adds on to something we already learned." I opened the book to page 11 and invited the children to read alongside me.

Tigers live on the continent of Asia. Some tigers live in forests.

I glanced to see if any thumbs were up, hoping to see some. I saw a few, but not nearly as many as I'd hoped, so I began to think aloud, "Hmm, . . . does this information add on to what we already know?" I said with bewilderment on my face, "This part is teaching us . . ." I waited to see if anyone was going to chime in.

"Tigers live in forests!" one student added as I ran my finger around the picture.

Yesterday readers took a sneak peek to notice parts that went together across books. Nudge readers to revisit these parts, rereading carefully with the intention of adding information to grow an even deeper understanding of a topic.

Be sure to select a main topic that is found across two texts. You'll want to be sure to have already read about the main topic in one text so that readers can recall what they already learned to accumulate information across books.

"Yes, it teaches us about where the tigers live." I moved my finger to the words and continued, "Oh! That's the same in this book!" I quickly shifted back to our original *Tigers* book, by Laura Marsh. I opened to the page where it taught about tigers living in forests and continued, "We learned that tigers live in forests that can be cold or hot, and they live near water." I pointed to our first book.

"Let's keep reading! Let's see what else we can add to what we know about tigers."

> *It is cold in some of the forests. There can be a lot of snow there. Other tigers live in swamps. It is warm in the swamps.*

"Turn and talk, what else are we learning about tigers here?" I circulated to listen.

"Some of you noticed things that were the same across your books. Dimitri noticed that both books taught that tigers live in hot places *and* in cold places. *And* he added on to his knowledge by noticing that the new book teaches that tigers live in swamps. It added on to what he already learned about tigers. It taught him about one kind of water they live near and swim in. Now that's what I call *adding on* to what you've already learned. Perfect-o!"

Provide a chance for repeated practice by comparing and adding information to a different part of the same text set.

"Let's keep reading and see if anything else makes us go, 'Ohhhh, that's the same!' Ready?" I flipped to page 15.

> *Female tigers have two to four cubs at a time.*

I looked out at the class and saw a couple thumbs. "Is this the same? What is this part teaching us?"

"About tiger babies!" one student said.

"Cubs! Tiger cubs!" another added.

"Tiger cubs! Ohhhh! We read a *whole* chapter on that in our *Tigers* book during shared reading! Let's keep reading our new book! What else can you add to what you know about tigers?"

> *At first, the cubs drink their mother's milk. Then she teaches them to hunt. The cubs leave their mother by the time they are three years old. Wild tigers can live for 10 to 15 years.*

"What else are we learning about tigers here? Turn and talk!

"Henry noticed that both books said that tiger cubs drink their mother's milk when they are born! Some of you noticed that our new book added that the mother tiger teaches the cubs to hunt! I also heard you say that our new book taught us that wild tigers live for ten to fifteen years!"

Rather than reading or rereading two passages from two different texts, quickly cite particular information from a previous text to help children recall those details and, now, add to that knowledge.

Be mindful of pace. Rather than calling on individual readers, invite students to turn and talk to notice what is the same and what is new, before naming back what you heard partners say. As you listen in, formatively assess how children are able to synthesize information across texts. If you sense that this work is difficult, bring the class together to offer more guided practice.

Debrief. Generalize the work students just did.

"Did you see how as we were reading, we didn't just *wait* for something to pop out at us, but we actively tried to find and see what was the same in both books, and we added on to what we already knew and learned about our topic? This works the same in your topics!"

LINK

Add a new strategy to the chart. Then encourage readers to keep deepening their knowledge of a topic by reading more and more books that go together.

"So, readers, you are going to get ready for workshop. There are a few things you need to have prepared before you read today. You need to have out a book about a topic that you remember best or the first book you read on the topic. And then you need the next books on that same topic, stacked up, out and ready to read! You will also need to have Post-its out, ready to mark places that go together so that you can *add* to what you already know."

"Esteban marked some spots in orange in a few of his books that teach about what sharks eat. Nadia marked in pink a couple parts in her books that taught about what turtles look like. Now they are ready to read across books to add to what they know."

You might decide to give readers a different color Post-it for each of the main topics they read about in the first book. Then they can use these Post-its to mark places that are similar across books. In this way, students can be prepared to add to what they already know.

Adding the new strategy to the chart, I faced the class with a sense of urgency to ask, "Are you ready to prepare for workshop and learn a lot about your topics? Are you ready to read book after book, devouring more and more information, to grow an epic amount of knowledge about a topic? Let's set up and start reading. Pip pip!"

Coaching Students to Use Replicable Strategies to Maintain Meaning

Confer with readers and coach them to actively bring their understandings back to the text.

You will want to identify the difficulties your readers may be having and support them with the steps that they need to move forward. As you confer with readers, check in to see how they are thinking about their books. You may ask them, "Here on this page, what kinds of questions are you thinking about?" Look to see which children are doing nothing more than saying back the facts and which are making something of what they read. You might teach readers who need this help to pose questions that are beyond just literal comprehension.

You may say, "As you read parts of your book, be asking yourself things like 'Why does that happen? How is that important? What is another example of that?'" You may even jot some of these questions on a Post-it and say to the student, "Let's read together, and after a bit, let's stop and raise some questions. I'll go first and then you can try."

You could then read a bit aloud, pose one of the universal questions you just mentioned, and show the child how you think about a possible answer to that question. It will be important that when you intervene like this, you do so to teach kids something they can do repeatedly, with any book, and not just to ramp up their thinking about the book at hand. That's why it is helpful to suggest a list of universally applicable questions, such as "Why does this happen?"

Of course, there is nothing magic about teaching kids to generate questions as they read nonfiction texts. That is just one of a lot of things you will have taught readers to do that could probably use spotlighting. But the bigger point is that it is important to make sure the work you do in one text is transferable to other texts. For example, after you confer with a reader to decode and define a tricky word, you'll want to back up and name what you and the reader just did. You might say, "Did you see that you did two things? You first figured out what the word actually said, and then, when you didn't know what it meant, you used the whole page and everything you know about

the topic to help you think that through." You might set the youngster up to practice this in more places by saying something like "I see that on the next three pages you have three more words to figure out. Could you do the same thing we did here? Look at this book in your baggie, the next one you were going to read. You can do that work on these pages as well!"

MID-WORKSHOP TEACHING
Marking Similar Parts to Learn More

"Readers," I interrupted, as I held up two books from Sarah, the student nearest to me, and continued, "It's great to see you looking back to your first book as you're reading your other books and figuring out how the books add on to what you've learned. Sarah was reading *Trains* and found a part that was talking about the history of trains. And then she remembered that her book about airplanes—guess what?—*also* had a part about the history of airplanes." I showed both sections under the document camera.

"Marcos was reading about butterflies, and he marked a part in this book that talks about the enemies of butterflies. Then he remembered that in his first book, there was *also* a part about predators of caterpillars and butterflies. So he opened *that* book and also marked it. The information in his other books added on to information in his first book. Look," I said as I showed his Post-it note that signaled his learning. "Oh yeah, *and* he said it was surprising to find out that birds were a predator, so he marked this spot as well." I showed the part he'd marked with a response Post-it. "That's big thinking, Marcos!

"After you read a section or a part, stop and recall what you've learned in other books. Does it fit together? Can you recall what you learned that was the same in other books? If the answer is yes, find those parts, mark those spots, and you'll be well prepared to talk and share all your knowledge with others."

Searching for Information that Goes Together

Send readers off on a learning scavenger hunt, banding with partners to talk about information that goes together.

"Readers," I began as the last student settled in and tucked his book baggie beneath him, "the year began and you grew like beanstalks. During these past few weeks, you've been growing knowledge about topics. Well, it's time for a little harvesting." I smiled and explained, "You know what a harvest is, don't you? It's when a farmer knows that his fields are full of vegetables and his orchard is full of fruit, and he collects it to share with others.

"In just a moment, you're going to harvest some of the information you've grown with your partner. You and your partner will fill a whole bushel basket full of information that goes together. Partner 2, you'll start today. Find a place in one of the books that really interested you, and read that part aloud to your partner. Then say what it makes you think. Then *both* of you can search and find other parts of books that in *some way* go with that first part. You might say things like this:

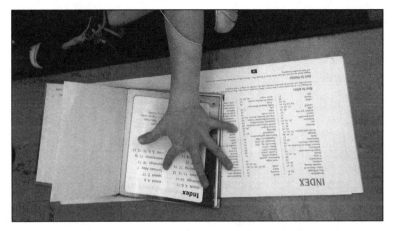

FIG. 13–1   A student uses the index to locate parts of different books that go together in some way.

"'I found more information about that. Listen!'

"'This book has an example of that. Listen!'

"'I know another place that talks about that. Listen!'

"After you are done with one topic, move on to a second one. Get to filling those bushel baskets full of knowledge. Work *together* as partners to add on and find some ways that your books go together."

Thinking and Rethinking about How Information Is Connected across Books

IN THIS SESSION, you'll teach readers how to connect information from more than one book that seems different by rethinking ways to categorize and name the information.

GETTING READY

✔ Find three photographs that go together in a way that isn't obvious. We use photographs of bears: one of a brown bear stripping a blueberry bush, another of a black bear catching salmon, and the third of a bear climbing a tree (see Teaching).

✔ Be ready to refer to passages in both demonstration texts to show how noticing differences can lead to similarities. We use page 19 in *Amazing Animals: Tigers*, by Valerie Bodden, and page 12 in *Tigers*, by Laura Marsh (see Active Engagement).

✔ Display the "Experts Grow Knowledge Across Books!" anchor chart on the easel so that it is ready to refer to (see Link). 👆

✔ Ask children to bring book baggies to the meeting area (see Share).

✔ Make copies of the "Ways to Say More" sheets for partnerships (optional) (see Share). 👆

MINILESSON

CONNECTION

Facilitate a quick game that gets kids talking about information that was similar when comparing texts.

The readers gathered together and I began, "Think about the kinds of things you found in a few of your books that added on to what you already knew about your topics. I am going to toss you an imaginary ball, and when you catch it, say what you found. When you are ready to tell, put your hands out, so I know you want to catch the ball and talk to us." I looked to see who was ready to catch the ball and tossed it to a student.

"Both of my books teach about frogs and hibernating," piped up Jonah, who tossed the ball back to me. I tossed it to another student.

Miguel said, "I found out that this is a loader truck." He turned the page toward me and pointed to the picture.

"Was that in both books?" I questioned.

"Yep, both books had loaders," he responded as he flipped pages and held up his second book.

The ball was tossed back to me and I tossed it out again. "In all of my books, it showed what plants need to survive," chimed in Megs as she caught the imaginary ball and joined the game.

As Megs tossed the ball back, I nodded to show my understanding and explained, "Some of you found *details* that were similar, and some of you found *whole parts* and chapters that were similar in a few books. Noticing the things that add on to what you know really, *really* grows your knowledge.

You aren't just growing like beanstalks," I said, hearkening back to our first unit of study, "your *knowledge* is growing like a whole farm full of beanstalks!

"Something else happened yesterday, though. *Many* of you found that your books didn't always seem to have parts that went together. You had books on the same topic—like planets—but the books didn't seem to have pages or parts that had much to do with each other. Like one book had information about all the different planets, and the other book was about Saturn's rings. When that happens, you don't just say, 'Nope, they don't match' and move on. You have to look again, read again, and think again."

❖ **Name the teaching point.**

"Today I want to teach you that when readers read a bunch of books on a topic, they sometimes think that nothing from one book goes with the other book. When that happens, readers know to look again and try a different way of naming what's going on."

TEACHING

Provide a quick explanation and example, using photographs, to demonstrate how noticing what is different can lead to what is the same.

"For example, I could look at these two photographs about bears." I put two photographs of bears onto the document camera, side by side. "When I look quickly, I might just see that one teaches me that bears eat blueberries and the other," I said, moving my finger to the second photo, "teaches me that some bears fish."

I paused and then said, "I suppose someone, who was just looking ho-hum, could say that these two photos don't go together. There aren't blueberries on both pages, there isn't even the same bear on each page. This one is black," I pointed to the bear in the first photo. "And this one is brown," I said of the bear in the river. "The photo of the bear doesn't add on to the blueberry-eating bear. No! They don't go together.

"*But* if I named the pages *in a different way* and really thought about what they both are teaching me, I could figure out how to put the pictures together to grow knowledge. I could say that both are about the same thing. What?" I trailed off for just a moment then said, along with many of my audience, "Eating! Exactly! Both are teaching about bears eating.

"Now, let's try something harder. Look at *these* two photographs. Look closely and really think about how to grow knowledge about these two photos. Think about how they go together to teach you." I left the photograph of the bear eating berries on the document camera, but I replaced the second photo with a picture of a bear climbing a tree.

"Let's try to say two things that are the same. I mean, we already can name—really quickly—that *both* have bears. But let's think about the two pictures *differently* to grow knowledge. Here the bear is doing something. It's climbing a tree. And here, the bear is also doing something. It's pulling those berries off the bushes and eating them. We could call both of these photographs, 'Things bears do.'

This opportunity offers students a chance to hear examples of how peers are doing this work of putting information together. It gives them ideas of things to look for more carefully in their own books. What's more, you'll get insight and a quick assessment of which students are categorizing information by topics and which students are still detail oriented.

You might choose to demonstrate this analogy using different pictures or a different animal you print from an online resource or display from other texts. You might even draw them yourself! Whatever route you choose, make sure to select images that can quickly make the point that sometimes what seems different can be put together to teach even more about a topic.

"Sometimes you have to search for different ways—*not* the most obvious way—to think about how things might be similar. It's hard work, but I know you can do it. Let's try with our tiger books."

ACTIVE ENGAGEMENT

Guide children to push their thinking when parts seem different, reading closely to consider what is the same.

"Let's think together about two parts in our books about tigers that at first glance don't seem to go together. We'll look again, in a different way, to think about and name what *is* the same. We will have to work hard to grow our knowledge by putting the two parts of the books together."

I opened to page 12 of *Tigers*, by Laura Marsh, and to page 19 of *Amazing Animals: Tigers*, by Valerie Bodden. I put page 12 on the document camera and began to reread:

> *Tiger Turf*
>
> *Besides hunting, tigers spend a lot of time marking their territory. They are not good at sharing!*
>
> *Tigers make long scratch marks on trees. They also rub their faces on trees and leave smelly scents. This tells other tigers to stay away.*

"Now this part!" I said, placing page 19 of *Amazing Animals: Tigers* under the document camera.

> *Tigers make different sounds. They can make a quiet "chuff" sound through their noses. They can growl and snarl, too. And they can roar very loud. Tigers may roar to tell other tigers to stay away.*

"It would be easy to say, 'Nope. The parts don't go together' or just, 'Both about tigers' and move on, but *don't* do it! Try harder. It might not be obvious. Try to think *differently* about these pages and how they fit together to help you grow knowledge. Study and think about them a different way."

Coach children as they discuss how parts fit together across texts.

I waited a moment while students studied the two pages, side by side. I could see students rereading and working out how to name how the pages went together. After a few moments, I had partnerships turn and talk to share their thinking.

I heard children telling each other how both pages taught how tigers do things to warn other animals about their space. What's more, I heard partnerships mention how the pages both taught about tiger moves.

After a bit, I interrupted, "Listen closely, readers. This partnership said that these pages are both showing ways tigers protect themselves. Is that true? Do you agree? Here they are marking their territory for tigers to stay away, and here they are growling and roaring to get other tigers to stay away." Heads nodded, and I continued.

Because the similarities are less explicit, it will be important to be transparent about how this skill requires careful reading and deeper thinking. It will also be helpful for students to have direct access to the pages and time to examine and discuss how they are alike in partnerships.

Listen into partnerships to assess if students are having difficulty. If it seems that they are having trouble making connections between the two parts, rally the class back together and think aloud how the parts can be put together to grow knowledge about the main topic.

"This partnership said that these two parts both show things that tigers are doing. Agree or disagree?" There was more head nodding and thumb raising to confirm thinking. "Whew! You are on the right track, doing the hard work of big-picture thinking. You're not just looking quickly and saying, 'Nope. Different,' and moving on. You're looking again, reading again, and thinking differently to understand how the books fit together."

LINK

Remind readers of what they've already learned but shouldn't forget to do as nonfiction readers.

"It's time to get ready to read. I know that some of you will be rereading about topics that you studied yesterday and the day before. Some of you may be starting new topics. Maybe your topics feel like old friends, or maybe they feel like complete strangers. Either way, remember what you need to do as a reader and a thinker to become an expert," I motioned to the chart and asked the kids to name each bullet. "I need to do a quick thinking check before I send you back to grow knowledge across the books in your baggies. Think about these things and, if they are true for you as a reader, give me an air check."

I began to read the chart, and students began to give their checks as I touched each bullet.

ANCHOR CHART

Experts Grow Knowledge Across Books!

- Notice parts that go together.
- Add to what you know.

"Now it's time to get ready to read. Stack those books, get your Post-its, and get to it!"

This is sophisticated work that readers may need extra coaching to do as they read independently. Compliment readers who are making less obvious connections to accumulate information across texts. You will also be surprised by the connections kids make, some even making connections across different topic sets. For example, one reader might discuss how owls protect themselves, while another might add that starfish do the same.

Coaching and Scaffolding Students' Comprehension

Gather a small group of students together and pull out all the stops to secure students' understanding of critical nonfiction reading skills.

Use the anchor charts you made throughout the unit to teach children how to self-assess and make certain they are doing all they can to completely understand their books and topics. Encourage readers to set new goals for themselves as they look at the strategies on your charts and talk about what they are both strong at as well as what they need to continue to practice and improve as they continue to move up the leveled library system. Perhaps you'll say to your students, "The only person who knows, who *really knows* what you need to do to get even stronger and smarter as a reader is *you*. Now's your chance to study yourself closely. Think about the reading you're doing: Does it sound as good as you know you can sound? Are you thinking as *big* as you know you can think? Are you talking the talk that only experts can talk? Make plans right now to set goals for yourself."

Remind a small group of readers to pause while they read and think about what they are learning.

Pull a small group to do a strategy lesson on pausing to accumulate new learning. You could start by saying, "Readers, you've been devouring your books like potato chips, and that is wonderful, but I'm here to help make sure you don't get an information stomachache. As you read, remember to not wait until the end to figure out what the author is teaching you. Pause *while* you read, quickly and often, and think about what you are learning about your topic."

You might practice together on a shared text first, having partnerships turn and talk to digest information. Remind readers that they'll do this work in their minds, and then coach them as they do this in their own books, moving from child to child and providing lean prompts as reminders to pause and think about what they are learning. You might also offer tips that move readers toward determining importance as they read, encouraging students to look back on and use features to help. "Look at that picture/diagram/heading," you might begin. "How do they all go together? What did this part teach you about the topic? What did you learn?"

Continue to facilitate small-group shared reading as a means of scaffolding instructional level texts for readers below benchmark.

Follow up with the readers who were part of your small-group shared reading. Whether you supported readers to navigate nonfiction, read with fluency, monitor at points of

---

MID-WORKSHOP TEACHING **Think Big! Learn Big!**

"Readers, as you are studying and rereading your books, thinking about how the information is helping you grow knowledge on your topic, you are looking across books to figure out how they go together and to add on to your knowledge. Remember, you want to think about the *big* things, not the teeny-tiny details. You wouldn't look at two parts of different books about trucks and say, "They are silver!" or "There are drivers in both trucks." That's teeny-tiny. When you read *across* books, you are thinking, 'What are the *big* things these books are teaching me?'

"Take a minute right now to try this work and make sure you are doing *big* thinking. Think about your topic and tell yourself what the *big* thing is that you're learning and growing knowledge about. Is it *big*, like how animals grow up or ways trees help us? Or, is it a tiny, tiny thing like 'This strawberry has seeds,' or 'That truck is silver.'? Put your thumb up if you are trying to think about something b-i-g." I checked to make sure that many thumbs were up and then continued, "Now, tell your thinking to the person sitting next to you. Person, if you agree that it's something *big*, then share *your* thinking, check that it's *big*, and then both of you can keep reading. If it *doesn't* feel big, try again. I am certain that you can do it!"

error, or actively engage with texts, reflect on how much support you gave readers previously and consider giving readers less scaffolding this time around. Prompt readers to work through areas of difficulty with more independence. It will be important to listen for how far individual readers are from their instructional level.

During their first interaction with a text at this level, you probably had to provide a lot of scaffolding, but you might find that your support is needed a lot less this time around. This exciting development might cause you to assess whether readers are ready to turn what was once their instructional level into their new just-right level. Listen as children scaffold the book for each other, and compliment them as they do so, giving explicit feedback about the moves they are making to both monitor and self-correct their reading as a team. Allow readers to have access to the book after you've read through it together to support the acceleration of their progress toward the next level and encourage these readers to practice with the book, rereading with greater accuracy, fluency, and comprehension.

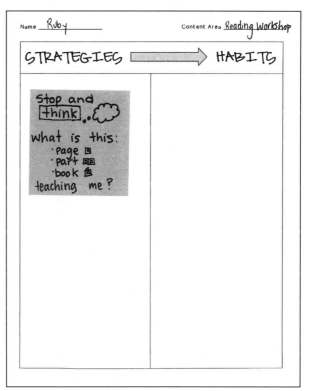

FIG. 14–1   These Strategies to Habits pages can help students hold onto the tangible artifacts you may have given during conferring and small-group work. It can remain in book baggies and help remind readers of their individual goals

Bolstering Talk by Using Examples from Books

Distribute talk prompts to support elaboration, and channel partners to say more about their topics by retelling their learning across books.

As the readers gathered in the meeting area today, I had a small stack of talk charts that I quickly distributed among partnerships. "Readers, you've been growing knowledge to put your books together and learn a lot about different topics. Let's share some examples with our partners! I gave you a talking chart to help you talk about how your books go together. Only use it if you need help talking to your partner, just in case.

I put the talk sheet under the document camera and read some of the prompts as I pointed to each on the page:

Ways to Say More

"Another example is . . ."

"This is the same because . . ."

"This book shows the same thing a little differently . . ."

"Right now, Partner 2, talk about a topic. Retell your topic, using information across your books. Give Partner 1 some examples of places where the information adds up!

"Partner 1, listen up! Maybe you've read some books on the *same* topic that your partner is now reading about. You might be able to give even more examples. Chime in and add, 'Oh! That's the same in my book because . . .' or 'I have another example to go with yours . . .' or 'My page or part is sort of like yours, but it's a little different because . . .'" I paused for just a moment then added, "Once Partner 2 is done, switch it up, and, Partner 1, get to retelling your topic."

FIG. 14–2   This Ways to Say More tool will support readers as they discuss their topics and retell their learning. You might use it in addition to the Readers Talk about Books chart from Unit 1.

Session 15

Finding, Thinking, and Talking about What Is the Same and What Is Different

MINILESSON

In the connection of your minilesson, consider explaining to children how readers notice and name differences as well as similarities. You might tell students, "Finding information that goes together is a *big* part of reading and learning about a topic. But readers can also grow knowledge about their topics by noticing and naming differences in their books as well. Reading is a lot like detective work. When you reread your nonfiction topics, you investigate, or read carefully part by part, to notice things that are different in your books."

You will then want to name the teaching point for your students by saying, "Today I want to teach you that when readers read a second or a third book on a topic, they start thinking about how this page and that page are sort of the same. They look really closely and see they are both the same *and* different."

During the teaching, you will want to demonstrate how to read for and notice differences to grow knowledge. You might direct children's attention to page 10 in *Tigers*, by Laura Marsh, and page 12 in *Amazing Animals: Tigers*, by Valerie Bodden. Remind the class that they read in both books about what tigers eat but also noticed that there are differences in the information. For example, Laura Marsh, in *Tigers*, gave examples of tigers eating deer and pigs, while Valerie Bodden, in *Amazing Animals: Tigers*, gave different examples of tiger food—monkeys and even (on occasion) people! Point out that both parts teach about what tigers eat, and then pivot readers to notice how the examples given were different and helped to grow knowledge and get a better understanding of tigers.

What's more, you could model how reading for differences helps a reader determine what an author thinks is important. (This helps build upon their last writing unit in narrative, *Lessons from The Masters*.) For example, you might consider whether *Tigers*, by Laura Marsh, cares more about tigers than *Amazing Animals: Tigers*. Use the example that shows how Laura devotes two chapters to teaching readers about caring for how tigers are doing today. On page 24, we learn about how and why tigers are in trouble. On page 28 we learn what we can do to help. On page 4 in *Amazing Animals: Tigers*, Valerie Bodden mentions that some tigers have died out but doesn't explain why or share ways we can help.

During the active engagement, invite readers to take out a set of their books and find similar parts. Then encourage them to reread closely, on the lookout for different information that will grow their knowledge. Voice over to partnerships to help them talk about differences and grow knowledge by saying, "Both of these parts were about . . . In this part I learned . . . , but that's different from the other book where I learned . . ." Be confident in knowing that when you push readers to think about the bigger ways that chapters and books are different, even if they are about the same topic, their knowledge is growing and deepening. Highlight readers who are doing this work to show how it might look within different contexts.

When you deliver the link, recap the options you practiced together in today's lesson. Remind children that they might notice differences that seem small, like the details in two parts that are about the same thing. Instead of asking for a thumbs up to see who is planning to practice the strategy, invite students to pop up with a quick hop.

Name the next strategy, such as how readers read on the lookout to uncover things that are different and are much bigger than just one detail. It might be the way the author feels about the topic or the way the information is organized in a specific part or the entire book. Again, ask students to pop up if they are heading off to try this work today. It might also be that one book has different parts that another book doesn't have. Encourage readers to mark these differences, no matter their size, with Post-its to show partners during today's share. Before leaving the rug, draw attention to the anchor chart and the new strategy that you have added.

> **ANCHOR CHART**
>
> Experts Grow Knowledge Across Books!
> - Notice parts that go together.
> - Add to what you know.
> - **Spot differences (big & small).**

CONFERRING AND SMALL-GROUP WORK

Then you will want to confer and pull small groups, paying special attention to your higher-than-benchmark readers, teaching them how to collect the information they've gathered across texts. In books that are levels M, N, and O, the text begins to demand that the reader not only think about main topics but also start to work on figuring out the main ideas of texts.

You will also want to support your students in growing their understanding across texts. Look for students who mostly just retell the facts or have a hard time thinking beyond the literal information in the text.

Gather these students together for a small group. You may decide to take out the book from Bend I, *Knights in Shining Armor*, by Gail Gibbons, and you might say to your students, "One way that can help you think about information to grow some knowledge and ideas about your topics is to raise important questions like Why? and How? Look at some jots I have made from our knights book: 'Why weren't there any girl knights?' and 'How did the boys and families feel about the boys needing to leave their families when they were only seven?' Here's my last one: 'How long did it take to build a castle?' Now these questions are really going to get me to think more as I reread and consider some of the answers."

Next you can have students read a page or two of *Knights in Shining Armor* with you, keeping your questions in mind as you read. Pause when you encounter information relevant to your questions, and give students a minute to turn and talk and grow ideas together. Then, you might say to your readers, "Let's try the same things in your books. I am going to step back and give you a few minutes. When I get back, you will share with your partner and try to reread and answer some of these questions! Then we will see what kinds of ideas we have grown." On the following days, you may not work in a group text but rather gather students together again and support them in their just-right books for the whole of the strategy lesson.

Mid-Workshop Teaching

During the mid-workshop teaching, warn readers that sometimes information is different because there are discrepancies across books. Explain that this means that two authors might actually say two different things. You might point out how in *Tigers*, the author tells us that female tigers usually have two or three cubs at one time, but the author of *Amazing Animals: Tigers* tells us that female tigers have two to four cubs at a time. Also in *Amazing Animals: Tigers*, we learn that cubs leave their mother by the time they are three. In *Tigers*, we learn that they are two years old when they leave to find their own territories. Celebrate if readers notice any discrepancies, because this is hard work to do. Remind second-graders that noticing discrepancies is yet another thing that readers do to grow knowledge and understand their topics, especially when reading and thinking across books.

SHARE

During the share, readers can bring any differences they noticed across their books. You will want to tell your readers that as they work in partnerships they should be listening and asking for evidence and proof about what their partners are thinking about and finding in their books. Coach partners to read aloud parts and sections that *show* and prove. Make sure that *both* partners are working together to clarify and grow ideas. Encourage partnerships to use words from the "Ways to Say More" talk prompt sheet, such as "This book shows the same thing a little differently . . ." and to keep the conversation going by questioning, "Why are these different? What's important about the differences?"

Readers Retell Topics, Not Just Books

IN THIS SESSION, you'll demonstrate how, after reading many books on a topic, readers put information together to retell the entire topic part by part instead of book by book.

GETTING READY

✔ Use both demonstration texts you have chosen. We use both *Tigers*, by Laura Marsh, and *Amazing Animals: Tigers*, by Valerie Bodden (see Teaching and Active Engagement).

✔ Display the "Experts Grow Knowledge Across Books!" chart and prepare to add the strategy "Retell topics (not just books)." to the chart (see Link).

✔ Ask readers to bring one set of books from their book baggies to the meeting area (see Share).

MINILESSON

CONNECTION

Tell a quick story demonstrating how experts put information across books together when sharing knowledge about a topic.

"Readers, the other day I took my youngest nephew to the zoo, and guess what we saw?" I said as I arched my thumb toward the two tiger books sitting on the easel.

"Tigers!" the children cheered in unison.

"Yes! We saw tigers. We were watching them through the fence when my nephew asked, 'Is he eating that plant?' So I was all, 'No, no, no, Henry. Tigers don't eat plants. They eat meat! They eat pigs and deer. Some even eat monkeys and—,' crouching down to look right at him I whispered, 'people!'

"Then he shouted, 'Oh, a baby!' and he jumped up and down a little.

"Henry, Henry, Henry,' I said. 'A tiger baby is called a *cub*. You should look around to see if there is another cub somewhere, because mother tigers usually have two to four cubs at a time. Look inside this territory to see where they are.'

"'What's a territory?' he asked.

"*You* know what territory is, but Henry is no tiger expert, so I explained it to him." I looked at the class, holding a book in each hand, and continued, "As I was teaching Henry about tigers, I realized that I was using information I learned from the different books at the same time!" I held up one book and then the other to make my point. "I wasn't retelling a book, I was retelling a *topic*. I put information from different books together to tell about the topic."

✦ **Name the teaching point.**

"Today I want to teach you that readers don't just retell the book; they retell the topic, using the words they own and all the information they have added together."

TEACHING AND ACTIVE ENGAGEMENT

Provide a quick nonexample to make clear that retelling a topic does not necessarily mean naming fact after fact after fact.

Waving the two tiger books high, I said, "Instead of retelling what happened in each book, you can think about *all* the knowledge you have grown and retell the *topic* instead. That means that you will want to retell the *big* things." Pointing to myself, I continued, "I'll start.

"When we retell, do we want to tell *every* little detail that we know about the topic? Like this," I said and took a dramatic, deep breath. As I exhaled, I began talking a mile a minute, rambling. "Tigers eat pigs and tigers have claws. Tigers are endangered and eat monkeys and they also have babies. Tigers live in Indonesia." I stopped, all out of breath. "Does that sound like I am retelling the big things or all the tiny, little things?"

"The little things!"

"You're right! I was *all over* the place, telling a little bit about one thing and then another. If you want to retell the *big* things about the topic, you need to start with thinking about the *parts* of the topic that you learned across your books."

Set readers up to try to retell the topic, this time considering the big parts of the topic and the information and examples that go with each part.

"Let's try to retell this topic in a sensible way, part by part by part. Think first about the different parts of the topic we learned about. Use your fingers to help. After you have some ideas, I want you to turn to your partner and retell each other the parts of the topic that you have remembered."

"Some of you said we learned about how tigers are in trouble." I touched one finger as I named the part. "We absolutely did! We learned a lot of information in *both* books on how tigers are endangered. Think about a detail from both books that goes with that part of the topic. When you have a couple of details, pop your thumb on your knee."

I waited a moment to make sure most thumbs were up before calling on a student to offer details that went along with tigers in trouble. The details matched that part of the topic, so I continued. "Let's keep going."

You'll notice that we purposefully do a nonexample here. This isn't the work we want our readers to do, but often, it is what second-grade readers do when trying to retell information. We want readers to retell the topic in an organized, knowledge-growing sort of way, retelling about a subtopic and supplying information and examples from across texts.

Readers will inevitably name details. When this happens, voice over to name main topics that house the details they are recalling. Continue to nudge readers to think of the bigger part, the main topic, before moving to detail-by-detail retelling. After the turn-and-talk, rearticulate the information in a more transferable way.

Allow time for repeated practice, guiding readers to continue to orchestrate the process of determining the next big part and the examples that match.

"Our next part about the topic of tigers is . . ." I looked around at the raised thumbs and asked Fiona to come up with a part of the big topic.

"Cubs!" she said proudly.

"This *is* another part of our big topic. Turn and give your partner a couple of important details we learned about cubs." Again, the students talked, and then I voiced over a couple of examples I'd heard.

"I notice how you are using the lingo of the book to think about the parts and the examples. One more try together, and then I'll send you off to get started on your own topics. Another part of the topic of tigers could be . . . ," I said, my voice trailing off to gauge engagement.

"What they look like," said Josie.

"Yes," I said. "Turn and talk to give some examples from the two books about that part of the topic."

After students gave a couple examples, I shared out a detail or two.

I then said, "Do you see how you are retelling the parts and giving one or two details or examples from the book. You aren't *all* over the place calling out random details you remember. First, you thought about the parts of the topic and then began to tell about each one—*almost* as if you were writing your *own* all-about book about tigers!"

LINK

Add the final strategy to the anchor chart, highlighting that because students have grown knowledge across books they can now retell topics like experts.

"Just like you have become tiger experts and can retell the parts of the big topic and details from both of our tigers books, I know you've become experts on other topics as well—experts on transportation and earthworms. Experts on birds and weather. You've *grown* knowledge about topics by reading and learning across books, and I just knew that you could . . ." I tapped the final point on the anchor chart and read it aloud.

Listen for readers who are still naming details, rather than the main topic. Continue to prompt readers to think about where the detail fits within the larger context of the topic. We've included opportunities for repeated practice, but you might have all students, or the ones who are specifically displaying difficulty, apply the strategy to one topic in their baggies right then and there. Remind readers to use features to help determine importance. You might say, "Use the table of contents to remember what the main topics are." If there isn't a table of contents, you might prompt, "How did the pages go together to teach about the topic part by part?" Later on, in the share, you'll offer the opportunity to practice yet again, inviting partners to retell topics to each other.

Whenever possible, help students make connections between the work they are doing in both reading and writing.

ANCHOR
CHART

Experts Grow Knowledge Across Books!

- Notice parts that go together.
- Add to what you know.
- Spot differences (big & small).
- **Retell topics (not just books).**

Retell topics
(not just books)

"The key is to retell the big things, the main parts of the topic. Then give an example or two to help show what is important to know and use keywords to talk the talk. Off you go. There is knowledge to grow and topics to retell and all sorts of reading to be done!"

Lifting the Level of Students' Thinking

Coach readers to do some close reading and inferential thinking as they read.

Reading comprehension is as thick as thinking itself: complex and nuanced. Each day you offer readers an opportunity to savor their thinking about texts, whether they are doing so on Post-its when they get to the end of a section or during a reread of a book or when talking with partners. There's no such thing as too much comprehension when it comes to understanding books. It's likely that today's conferring and small-group work will be focused on lifting the level of student thinking and talk. Plan to work with a variety of readers today as you meet in individual conferences with both your striving and struggling readers. You'll want to help readers put together parts across one text to understand the main topic of their book and also be sure they are thinking across their texts. While some students may find things that are similar and different, other students may be working on comparing things such as an idea or an opinion or a point that the texts are trying to make.

In addition to conducting conferences, you may consider bringing together a small group of readers who'll benefit from repeated practice and immediate coaching or feedback while practicing how to talk about a topic across books. With these students, consider having them pick a part of their topic that they'd like to grow knowledge about across books and name that part. For example, a reader might be reading about sports and decide to grow knowledge about the Olympics. If readers name a smaller detail, nudge them to consider the larger part or category into which that particular information would fit. For example, if a child says that monkeys eat bananas, prompt her to see how that information might fit into the larger category of what monkeys eat and to see how to keep her big idea in mind as she reads across books—using features such as tables of contents and indexes to find and read information effectively and efficiently.

Once children have identified a part or category of their topic, encourage them to reread closely across books, looking for examples and details that go with that specific part. Remind children that as they read and learn information, they need to think about how it is important to the bigger topic. As kids read more and more books with a specific lens, prompt them to be flexible learners, checking in with themselves often to say, "Yes, I already knew this," or "Cool! This adds to what I already knew!" or "Wait, this is different!" Don't shy away from having readers take time to mark a page or stop and sketch or do a quick jot about their thinking and understanding as they read. Provide Post-it notes for these purposes. You might suggest that students use a symbol system to support their thinking (for example, a star to confirm what a reader already knows or an explanation mark to note new information learned) as they grow knowledge.

Then you may pull a small group of readers who are reading higher-level texts to help them think about finding points and angles that the authors may be trying to show in their books. Have a few texts ready where authors make this work clear. You may say to your students, "Sometimes authors take different sides about the information they are teaching. In this book about storms, the author explains that storms can be both destructive and helpful. When she explains that sandstorms can knock fences down, it makes me think that storms are destructive. When she says that wind helps clean our air, it makes me think that storms can be helpful." Then encourage and support

MID-WORKSHOP TEACHING Readers Don't Just Get Ready to Read, They Also Get Ready to Retell

"Readers, to retell your topics well, it helps to do the same work you did to get ready to read about your topic. Spread out all your materials to remember the parts, asking, 'What are the big parts of this topic? What are the main parts of the big topic in this book?' You can peek at the table of contents, flip through the pages of your books, and reread. Then, practice retelling parts of the big topic and naming an example or two that goes with each part. Don't forget to use all the lingo you've learned to talk the talk!"

readers as they look for words and pictures that help show the varying angles of their topics. Coach your kids to keep quick jottings on what they are learning. Teach readers to question their ideas about information, asking, "Is that always true?"

Remind readers to continue using habits from the last unit of study as well as the habits they developed earlier in this unit.

Although part of your teaching will be aimed at supporting the new work of the bend, you will also want to help students do all that they've been taught thus far—and to do so with orchestration. Too often, children treat reading strategies like magic tricks, pulling one out of their cap and not realizing they can use the strategy again and again to think deeply and grow knowledge. Show readers how to use the anchor charts as repertoire—not ordering one item, but putting strategies together to do as much thinking and understanding as possible about their topics. For example, some children will need reminders to monitor their reading around vocabulary understanding and usage, so you might help students revisit the "Talk the Talk! Read to Learn the Lingo!" chart as well as put together the parts of books. You may say, "Don't forget to figure that word out and then go back to read it smoothly and sound like an expert! Let's try that right now!"

Nudge students to come up with ideas for when they finish a book and stop. Hopefully, they will say, "I need to do something!" You can then ask, "What will you try?" You may even need to help the students make a short list of three choices to choose from each time they finish a book.

Letting Partners Retell to Teach Each Other

Channel partnerships to retell one of their topics to one another, reminding students to retell part by part.

"Experts, now is the time to put all this retelling work into action to teach your partner about your topic. Partner 1, you'll go first. Get out the books that go with one of your topics. Think about the big parts and give some examples that go with each part. Get started!"

As partners began to retell, I moved around the room coaching students to add more details, using the books to find and show examples. I prompted, "Use your book to help you remember the parts," and "Flip back and forth between your books as you retell."

I also coached by saying, "Show a picture or a feature," and "Reread a few sentences like an expert to say more." In addition to coaching into their talk, I reminded partnerships to use their keywords to talk the talk of their topics.

Coach students to listen attentively to grow knowledge.

What's more, as I moved between partnerships, I reminded students to listen attentively to grow knowledge. I said, "Partner 2, lean in close and listen carefully. You might even ask a question! You can become an expert, too, just by listening!"

After a few minutes, I called students back to celebrate. "Partner 1, well done! Being an expert is hard work. Partner 2, get ready. Take out the topic you're going to retell. Partner 1, don't forget you'll be listening to grow knowledge. Stop to say what you're thinking or wondering!" Again, I moved around the rug to coach students as they retold their topics part by part.

Session 17

Getting Ready for the Celebration

MINILESSON

CONNECTION

Uncover a letter from the book fairy with exciting news: a request to transform the classroom into a museum packed with exhibits visitors will come to grow knowledge from.

"Readers, yesterday we thought about how we could retell topics, not just books." I picked up our two tiger texts for all to see and gave each book a tiny, intentional shake so that from inside one of the pages, an envelope fell out. "To the Experts of 2-202" was written on the front. Some kids gasped. Others looked with wide eyes at each other. The class was confused and excited: "It's a letter!" "Read it!" "Who's it from?" erupted from the students in the meeting area.

Ripping open the envelope I unfolded the letter, smoothing it against my lap. The conversation turned to silence as eager eyes watched and waited to hear who had sent the mysterious letter. I cleared my throat and began to read:

> Dearest Experts,
>
> Greetings! I'm so pleased that you've received the books I've left you. It's clear that you've been working hard to learn all that you can this month. I do hope you've enjoyed reading the books as much as I enjoyed delivering them to you.

"It's from the book fairy!" the children squealed with delight.

"I do believe you're right. How incredible, but, wait, there's more!" I read down the page:

> I am writing to ask one thing in exchange for the gifts I have given you. As experts, you have a great responsibility to give your gift of knowledge to others.

IN THIS SESSION, you'll announce that the book fairy has returned, this time with an assignment to create exhibits where children will soon take on the role of tour guides, teaching visitors about topics they have grown knowledge about.

GETTING READY

✔ Type a letter from the book fairy. Come up with your own or use ours for inspiration. Seal it in an envelope and address it to your class (see Connection).

✔ Display on the easel the demonstration texts you have been using. We use *Tigers*, by Laura Marsh, and *Amazing Animals: Tigers*, by Valerie Bodden (see Teaching).

✔ Gather some Post-its and markers to use to demonstrate how children can help plan an exhibit (see Teaching).

✔ Create two different booklets using pages from both demonstration texts. Set it up so that each booklet contains information about different parts of the topic from both texts. For example, one booklet might contain information from both books about what tigers eat and another booklet might contain information about where tigers live (see Active Engagement).

✔ Ask children to bring their book baggie to the meeting area (see Link).

✔ Display the "Talk the Talk! Read to Learn the Lingo" anchor chart from Bend II (see Conferring and Small-Group Work). 👏

I ask that you pay it forward and teach others what you know. Transform your classroom into a museum, a place where people can visit to grow knowledge about many things. Each of you can be a tour guide of your very own exhibit, teaching visitors all that you know about your topic. I do so hope you'll agree.

Kindest tidings,

The Book Fairy

"Are we up for the challenge?"

I heard cries of, "Yes!" as well as, "We can do it!" "I'll be a tour guide!" chimed a voice, eagerly accepting.

❧ **Name the teaching point.**

"Today I want to teach you that to teach in ways that get others to learn a lot, you need to be prepared. You can mark the parts, think about what you want to say, and use your voice to help people listen and learn a lot."

TEACHING

Play the role of tour guide to teach all about the class topic. Recruit students to watch closely, noticing the moves you make as a tour guide.

"Okay, I am going to start to give you a tour of tigers. Will you watch to see how I have marked places and ideas to teach, and notice the way I use my voice to help you listen and learn a lot?"

I sat up in my seat, straightening my posture as if to convey a certain seriousness. "Ahem, welcome! Let me teach you about tigers. Tigers are magnificent cats. They are actually the biggest cats in the *world*."

I heard a few giggles from the children as I held up a finger. "One important thing you should know about tigers is what they look like." I looked back at the class, shifting my voice from that of a tour guide to an aside addressing the children.

"Oh! I think this is the perfect place to show a picture! Hmm . . . what might be a good picture or page to show?" I picked up *Tigers* and began to skim through it. Stopping on page 8, I held the book up for everyone to see. "*This* page really shows what tigers look like. Maybe when I teach, I can point to parts of this page. Watch how I do this."

Demonstrate how you change your voice to match the content you are teaching.

I tapped the picture that displayed a tiger's coat and said, "One thing you should know about how tigers look is that their coat has stripes that help camouflage it in the grass." I paused before resuming my regular voice and whispered, "I should change my voice now to match what I'm about to say." Continuing my tour guide bit, I slowed and tensed my voice to say, "This helps tigers hunt so that its prey won't see it coming."

Play up the dramatics! Read the letter slowly, pausing to glance up at the class and gauge their excitement. As you move into the teach, keep the theatrics going as you model the role of tour guide for the class. The engagement you build in this connection will help sustain students as they prepare for the unit's celebration.

As the teaching progresses, you'll offer children tips to lift the level of their exhibit. You'll show students that they can determine what pictures to show, the voice or voices they'll use to teach, and the order of the main topics that one might move through.

I broke character to exclaim, "I'll just mark this part, with a number 1, because I think I am going to start by talking about that on my tour. And I'll write 'quiet voice' so I remember how to read it. Being a tour guide is so much fun! We can pick the big parts and the examples we'll want our visitors to know."

Debrief. Name the important work you demonstrated.

"Did you notice I thought about what to mark and teach first? And how I used my voice to talk to you as an expert tour guide? You can decide the pictures and the voice that will make your exhibits top-notch! Okay, tour guides, help me keep this exhibit going. You be the tour guides."

ACTIVE ENGAGEMENT

Divide booklets containing copied pages about a single topic from both tiger texts across partnerships to practice the role of tour guides.

I picked up the stack of booklets and explained, "You're going to practice being tour guides together before you go off and practice on your own and with your own topic!" I passed out booklets so that Partner 1s and Partner 2s were holding different pages, and then I continued, "Look through the pages and prepare to teach others. Think about which part you would mark, and choose the examples you'll mention, the pictures that you'll show to help explain, and the voices you'll use to teach so that our visitors can listen and learn a lot! Just a few more seconds. Now, turn and be tour guides!"

LINK

Invite readers to select the topic they'll want to be tour guides of. Then, encourage students to anticipate the information about their topic, the big parts and small examples, that they'll want their visitors to know.

"All right, tour guides, you've got some work to do to get prepared for the tours that you will be giving tomorrow! Look through your topics, reread some of your books, and make some choices. First, decide what topic you'd like to do."

I gave partners a minute to look through their baggies before saying, "Then, think about the big parts you'll want to teach. Reread those parts today and think about the examples you'll share from each part. Then mark some pictures that your visitors will need and jot down the kinds of voices you might use to get them to listen and learn a lot!

"When you have selected your topic, you can get started on the reading and preparations for your tours, which you will be giving tomorrow. Don't worry. At the end of today, you will have a practice run with your partners!"

You'll want to move around the room, offering light suggestions and affirmations as children make choices about the examples, pictures, and voices they would use in the assumed role of tour guide.

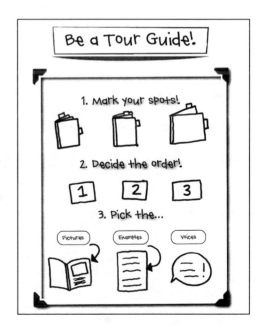

FIG. 17–1 You might offer students a mini-chart, such as this, to support them in the process of setting up their exhibits.

Supporting Preparation for the Celebration

Move from reader to reader, checking in on their plans for tomorrow's celebration.

You'll want to coach students as they reread and make plans for their final celebration tomorrow. Not only will this ensure that children feel confident and ready, but you'll also be supporting the ongoing work of orchestrating the many nonfiction skills unpacked across the unit. To cover more ground, consider working with one table of students at a time.

As children reread, you may decide to be a "perfect partner" to your students, giving them a chance to rehearse and practice being tour guides about their topics. As you listen, act like another second-grader might. Then give some feedback about how the readers could be more engaging, either with their voice or the examples that they collect, or even the way that they physically use the pages to teach.

You might also provide support as students continue to put together all that they have learned about reading nonfiction. As children retell their topics, prompt to help them determine the big parts of their topic first, looking across books and marking parts that go together. Then encourage readers to mix and match examples and information across books. You might ask, "What did you learn about what and how butterflies eat in *this* book? Did your *other* book say more about that? Let's open to both of those parts!" Prompt students to reread each part asking, "What am I learning about butterflies' eating in both books?" Remind students not to retell every single bit of information from each book but instead to name the big part they are retelling and to provide a couple of examples to go with each part.

Encourage students to use keywords as they retell and to explain how the words help us understand something key about the topic. If it seems that children are still unclear about the meaning of certain words, refer to the anchor chart from Bend II, "Talk the Talk! Read to Learn the Lingo!" and prompt readers to recall the many strategies they can utilize to figure out unfamiliar vocabulary.

MID-WORKSHOP TEACHING
Using Gestures to Bring Information to Life

"I just had an idea for another way to keep the audience's attention and make sure they're really listening. Don't just *say* the information. *Show* it. Use your body to show the shape, size, or movement to help your audience understand the information even better. You might even ask your audience to act it out with you! Try it right now. Think about a detail you might act out. How might you *show* it?"

Rehearsing Together for the Museum Opening!

Create a sense of urgency, calling readers to give each other feedback as they practice the role of tour guide on the eve of the big day.

"Partners, tomorrow is the big day! Close your eyes and picture it: visitors will come to *our* classroom, which will be transformed into a museum. They'll stroll from student to student, just like they were visiting special exhibits at a museum. They will listen and learn from all of you! Let's use these last moments to practice being tour guides. Take turns.

"Set up your exhibits and practice being tour guides for each other *before* our visitors come! Let's help each other get better! Whisper tips that will help to make your partner's exhibit the talk of the school! 'Show another picture!' you might say! 'Change your voice. Sound more serious!' 'Act that part out!' 'Give another example!'"

FIG. 17–2   Partnerships try on the role of tour guide to give each other feedback prior to the "museum opening."

Celebration
Pay It Forward by Teaching Others

IN THIS SESSION, you'll teach readers that they can keep visitors engaged by initiating questions about their topics.

GETTING READY

✔ Before class, send invitations to various classrooms. You might ask the classrooms to come at different times (one at 10:15, another at 10:25, a third at 10:35, and so on). Be brave. Send invites (or an Evite) to even the oldest children in your school. Invite those fifth-graders back down to the second-grade wing.

✔ Cue up the link to the "A Day in the Life, Museum Curator" video https://www.youtube.com/watch?v=4qCDSPe2-uc to 1:07 (search terms: day life curator Denver video) (see Connection). 👆

✔ Distribute two small stacks of Post-its (various colors). We use orange and blue. Make a demo. Draw a question mark on one color Post-it and a surprised face on the other color.

✔ Make sure children have the text set they want to read aloud and teach from, marked with Post-its to enhance their tour guide talks (see Active Engagement).

✔ Tie and tape an extra-wide, grand opening, celebratory red ribbon outside your doorway (if you have oversize scissors, use them, or better yet, have a bin of scissors ready for each student to help with the ribbon cutting).

✔ Construct Tour Guide buttons for each student. We improvised and used fancy-shaped Post-its and double-stick tape. Let each tour guide add his or her name and area of expertise to the name tag.

✔ Distribute a small stack of brightly colored paper and pens for visitors to leave comments (see Share).

MINILESSON

CONNECTION

Show students a video clip to illustrate the powerful work tour guides do.

"Tour guides, look what I found when I was thinking about how best to help you prepare for your exhibits today!" I cued up the "A Day in the Life, Museum Curator" video I found from the Denver Art Museum. "It's about a tour guide! Will you watch and see what she has to do to get ready for her museum's exhibits?" I pushed Play and let the video play for a couple minutes, then stopped and turned back toward the class. The kids were excited.

"Turn and tell your partner some of the things that the tour guide said she has to do to get ready for an exhibit!"

I heard a lot of ideas, such as "Make stuff for people to see" and "Get ready." I heard, "Decide what you want to tell," from a third voice. After a moment, I interrupted.

Name the big work the tour guide did that students can also do.

"Geez, Louise," I said. "She said so many of the same things that you've already done to get ready to give tours of your topics! You've reread and thought about the *big* information you'll teach. You've marked places in your books where you'll show your visitors what you've learned." I ticked each item off on a finger as I listed the work they did yesterday. Then I leaned close and continued.

"She also mentioned that she especially makes sure that people *learn* from her exhibit. She does things to prepare, and she thinks about how she'll make the exhibit a place where others can learn a lot. Let's make sure, right now, that *we* do that same work. Let's make sure that when we give our visitors a tour of our topics, we make sure that they *learn* all they can!"

❖ Name the teaching point.

"Today I want to teach you that to help your visitors learn all that they can, you will want to ask *them* questions about the things that you taught! Then you *and* your visitors can work on answering those questions to help them grow more knowledge about your special topic!"

TEACHING

Demonstrate how you rehearse for a tour of your topic, and show how you weave in a question for your audience to think about.

"So, let's work on this in our workshop. Visitors are coming today during the share time. You have just enough time to put the final touches on your information exhibit. Today's workshop is going to be a bit like a dress rehearsal, a practice before the real tour begins.

"First, *you* will act like my visitors, and I'll take you on a tour of tigers. Watch how I give the tour, and notice how I ask you some questions about what I just taught. Then I will help you answer them if you need it! Listen." I sat up and got started, using a clear, confident tour guide's voice.

"Hello, welcome to the tigers exhibit. You've chosen to learn about the biggest, the fiercest, and one of the most interesting cats in the whole world—tigers. Tigers are quite magnificent. First, let me teach you a bit about how a tiger looks. Their coats are striped, and no two tigers have the same stripe pattern." I showed the class the picture we'd marked yesterday in the minilesson, "and they have the biggest and sharpest teeth. Their teeth are sharp to help them tear through their prey's hide. Tigers also have claws that are sharp. They keep those claws sharp by sharpening them on trees."

I paused, "Now watch, I'm going to stop my tour and make sure my audience is learning from my exhibit. I'm going to be the kind of tour guide that asks a question so you can answer it and we can talk about it." I straightened back up and continued in my tour guide voice, "What do you think about the way tigers look?"

Name the transferable work you just modeled.

Leaning in, I said in my normal teacher voice, "Did you catch how I did that? I told about my topic. I gave you time to listen and learn, and then I marked a spot to remember to stop and make sure you were learning. I asked a question to help you grow more knowledge."

ACTIVE ENGAGEMENT

Set partnerships up to serve as tour guides. Support students as they teach and question their partner.

"Now it's your turn to try it. You can get started on the rug for just a moment, and then you'll get more rehearsal during reading time today."

FIG. 18–1 Post-its mark spots for readers to react and question.

Physically put a Question Mark Post-it on the book to mark the spot. Do the same with the Surprising Information Post-it to model how to prepare spots for stopping and talking during students' presentation of their exhibits.

"Partner 2, you'll start by being the tour guide. Give Partner 1 a tour of just the first thing you want to share and then stop to ask a question to make certain your partner is learning. Partner 1, listen closely, because Partner 2 is going to make sure you are learning! Then, the two of you can talk it out together. Okay, Partner 2, turn and tour talk." Pages turned and Partner 2s were off, teaching and questioning.

I listened in as Rosa taught her partner about blizzards. "Blizzards are a kind of super storm. That means the storm is extra big and strong! Just because it's snowing doesn't mean it's a blizzard. Blizzards have snow *and* wind *and* even can have tornadoes inside!" When she paused, I coached in, "Now, Rosa, ask a question to make certain Jeri's learning."

Rosa thought for just a moment then asked, "Why are blizzards super storms?" She'd just taught lots of information about what makes a blizzard a type of super storm, and her question matched that part of the topic. I named that for her and said to Jeri, "Did you see what Rosa did?" Turning to Rosa, I said, "You asked a question that really fit with the part you told about your topic. That's a great kind of question to ask." I gave her two thumbs up and moved on to another partnership, one where the preparation wasn't transferring so smoothly, and offered my support.

LINK

Rally students to make the most of every minute to prepare for their tours.

"Readers, to best prepare for our museum opening, let's head off and do some partner work. Rehearse your tour. I'll give you a bit of time to work with your partner, and then I'll make sure you switch, so the other partner gets to practice. That way you'll be able to practice at least twice. Remember that when you are touring people through your topic, you can ask them questions, listen to their answers, and talk it out together. Use your books when you talk it out.

"The countdown to the museum opening is on! Off you go."

FIG. 18–2 Partnerships use Post-its to organize and practice giving a tour of their topic.

Listening In and Coaching Readers to Be Tour Guides

IT'S LIKELY that today's conferring and small-group work will be made up, mostly, of listening in as readers rehearse, reread, and prepare for the upcoming celebration. You'll more than likely move fluidly from one partnership to another, coaching in, offering tips to make the exhibits more dramatic. You might hear yourself suggesting, "Don't just retell and reread. Be the kind of tour guide who acts parts out using your face and body—especially if you're trying to teach about a key word or new information."

You'll probably want to support students in being more informative as they retell their topics and share their learning with others. You may say something such as "Don't forget to tell the important information and some key details, not every single teeny, tiny nugget of information. Use your hand to hold the main topic, and tell the details across your fingers. Make sure all the details go with the main topic in your hand."

What's more, you'll coach students to use their voice to be a smooth-sounding tour guide and a more fluent reader, "C'mon, Sam, scoop those words—three- and four-word scoops' worth," or "Read it again. That's the ticket." You'll remind readers to remember to monitor by saying, "Ask yourself, 'Does that sound better?'" And of course you'll confirm and celebrate victories as readers rehearse by saying, "You're getting it, keep it up!"

And, of course, sprinkle in reminders and reteaching of talking the talk of nonfiction readers. "Jack, remember, you're an expert on this topic—use words to teach that sparkle and dazzle your learners. If they look confused, give them a little definition or use the book to show them what the words mean."

Along with your coaching and teaching, offer compliments that stick long after your conference. You might tell a partnership, "You're using your voice to talk like an expert. I can tell you feel confident about this topic because you can talk confidently about it," or "Wow, I admire how you reread and think about the *big* ideas you want to teach others. I could see you thinking carefully about where to mark your texts to get your visitors to be interactive. Rereading helps you sound better, and it helps you grow knowledge."

The goal here is to move quickly, listen in, and respond to make your readers feel both confident and connected to their reading. Support your readers and soon-to-be tour guides, and keep the atmosphere celebratory.

MID-WORKSHOP TEACHING
Taking Time to Teach, Taking Time to Listen

"We're getting closer to the opening of our museum, but right now, it's time to switch it up! Partners, take about ten seconds to decide who will give the first tour. Put your thumb up in the air so that I know who is doing the first tour and that you are ready." I waited to make sure the class was with me and then continued, "I can hear the thoughtful questions you are practicing for your visitors. Well done.

"But I just realized something, and it's too big not to teach you now. For visitors to learn *a lot*, we should make sure that *they* are *also* asking questions. You can listen to the questions *they* have and answer them. Use your book to show where you got the information.

"You know what that means, don't you, partners? As you are listening and learning, make sure that *you*, too, are thinking about some questions for your tour guide that go with the information that you are learning. Get to it. Tick-tock says the clock. Our museum doors will be opening soon!"

Celebrating the Hard Work of the Unit

Launch students into their official tours, creating a celebratory tone with pins, countdowns, and red ribbons to cut.

"Tour guides, the time has arrived. You've worked so hard to learn a lot, to talk the talk, to walk the walk. You have definitely learned and *earned* the title of tour guide. Let's put on our official tour guide pins, get ready for the opening, and have a countdown. We'll line up by the door, and as visitors arrive, you'll be able to lead them—just like a tour guide in a museum—to your exhibit. Okay, Partner 1, you line up on the right side of the door. Partner 2s, you'll line up on the left. Let's count down starting from ten, and then we will officially cut the red ribbon and we will be open for business. Ten, nine . . ."

When we reached one, the ribbon hung on both sides of the door, and the second-graders led visitors to their various exhibits in pairs and triads. There was much teaching and questioning and listening and growing of knowledge—and joy. A day well worth the wait.

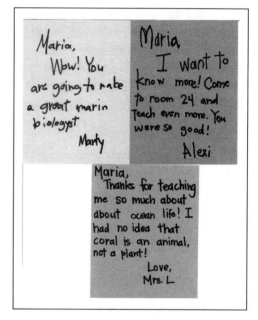

FIG. 18–4 Comment cards left behind by visitors for your tour guides to reflect on and celebrate their learning.

FIG. 18–3 Students celebrate the knowledge they have grown by creating exhibits that teach others about a topic.

Read-Aloud

Getting Ready: BOOK SELECTION

You will want to choose a text that will not only be of interest to your students but will help them practice and think about the essential reading skills needed to help them grow new knowledge. Your interactive read-aloud sessions across this unit should expose children to texts that are rich with information and provide opportunities for students to find main topics, navigate and understand domain-specific vocabulary, raise questions, and seek answers, as well as synthesize the information that they are learning.

In this unit, find books to read aloud that will set your students on fire about being curious and inquisitive and that will support children in feeling the awe and wonder that goes along with learning about a new topic. Book selection is of the utmost importance because you want your readers to be engaged, delighted, and excited about talking and thinking together. We selected *Knights in Shining Armor*, by Gail Gibbons, for several reasons. First, the text is above the end of the year benchmark. We suggest you take more than one day to unpack it with your students. While your shared reading is aimed at giving students access to texts just slightly above their independent reading level, you'll want your read-aloud text to be much more complex. *Knights in Shining Armor* is a level O text; thus, it offers second-grade readers opportunities to hear and

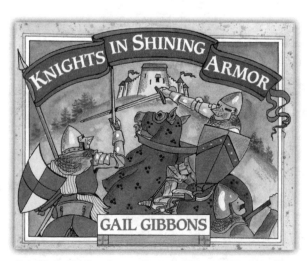

Knights in Shining Armor, by Gail Gibbons. Illustrated by Gail Gibbons.

learn rich vocabulary, grow knowledge, and understand information outside of known content. Most importantly, we chose *Knights in Shining Armor* because, in our opinion, it covers a topic that many of your students will enjoy yet might not pick up on their own. Your students will be reading about a wide variety of topics. Your read-aloud will be an example of how to think inside of books, regardless of topic.

We suggest you read this book aloud at least once during Bend I as a way to introduce students to many of the essential reading skills that will weave across the unit. You will find that *Knights in Shining Armor* is used a few times within the unit, but the sessions do not rely on students' familiarity with the entire text. Additionally, you will want to select other nonfiction books to read aloud to your students as the unit progresses. Look for texts with the same complexities as *Knights in Shining Armor*, and search for topics that will engage your young readers.

SESSION 1

BEFORE YOU READ

Introduce the new read-aloud to students. Build excitement and activate prior knowledge.

Call students to the rug and ask them to sit next to their reading partners. Introduce your new read-aloud. You might start your book introduction by saying, "Second-graders, I have a new book for us to read together. I'm so excited I can barely sit still. I found this book, *Knights in Shining Armor*, by Gail Gibbons, in the library. I picked it up and thought, 'I bet my second-graders would love to grow some new knowledge about knights from the olden days!' Do some of you have information you *already* know about knights? Wonderful! Some of you do and some of you don't. I bet *all* of us will learn new things as we read and think together!"

If you have already introduced Knights in Shining Armor *in Session 3 of Bend I, ask the children to recall what they did to take a sneak peek and to share what they remember about the book.*

Take a sneak peek. Think aloud as you preview the front and back covers, using the details from the pictures to anticipate main topics the book might teach.

"Let's take a sneak peek and make predictions about what Gail Gibbons might teach us. Will you look with me at the front and back covers and think, 'What will this book teach me?'" Then, you might think aloud and voice over predictions as you study the front and back covers, noticing and predicting what you will learn.

Page numbers are cited using the first page of text, starting with "The period known as the Middle Ages, from 500 to 1500 A.D., was also the Age of Knights."

Pages 1–3: Model how you preview a few pages in the text, lingering on illustrations to predict what the book will teach.

As you preview the first few pages, point to the details in the illustrations to channel readers to look closely. You might pause on a page and say, "This page is full of details. I'm noticing this person with a shield and sword, sitting on a horse. The horse is wearing clothes, too, look!" Point to each detail as you name what you notice. "From the illustrations on these pages, I predict that part of our learning will be about what knights used and how they dressed."

If you have taught Sessions 1 and 2 from Bend I, your students will already be familiar with pages 4–5, which show the diagram of a castle.

Pages 6–7: Invite students to join you in previewing the text, studying illustrations closely in partnerships.

Continue previewing the text. You might encourage the class to use details from the illustrations to try making their own predictions.

Open the text to pages 6–7, and display it so students can see. "What else do you see? Study the illustration alongside me and make some predictions. Put a thumb up when you are ready to turn and tell some predictions to your partner." After students have closely studied pages 6 and 7, have them turn and predict.

Listen in to students' responses to quickly assess predictions. You might use the following as a checklist as you listen to students discussing the text.

- ◆ Are students only noticing details and not doing the work of noticing details *and* predicting?

- ◆ Are students anticipating the information that this specific part will teach about the larger topic?

- ◆ Are students grounding their predictions in the information gleaned from the pictures, as well as their prior knowledge?

As you listen to students name what they notice and predict, you might voice over what you hear to the class at large, so other students hear strong examples of predictions based on a close study of illustrations. "I heard some of you noticing that these people look too young to be knights. You noticed that the boys are children and it looks as though they are training. Some of you predicted that this part might teach us about how young men became knights. Let's start reading to confirm your predictions and grow some knowledge about knights."

AS YOU READ

Pages 1–3: Read aloud the text with expression. Invite students to think about the text to understand its meaning.

From the start, read in an engaged and informative voice, taking in the parts of the page—the pictures, the captions—before reading the text. You might use your finger or zoom in using the document camera to study details in the illustrations, naming what you notice.

Coach students to think about meaning and monitor for comprehension. Students may be familiar with the topic, but there will be a lot of new information for them to understand to grow even more knowledge about the topic, and you'll want to give students opportunities to practice thinking about the information they are absorbing. To do this, you might say, "So we're learning a little bit about who knights were. A knight's *whole* life was based on fighting! Why would anyone want to become a knight?" Then you might reread page 3 before thinking aloud: "So I'm learning that the feudal system meant that if a knight protected his ruler, he would get land and money and people to work for him. Now I'm beginning to understand why someone would become a knight. Thumbs up if it's starting to make sense to you, too!"

Pages 6–7: Read the next few pages. Listen in to assess how well students are able to retell information they have just read. Then, model a proficient retell of the text.

After you read, you might prompt partners to turn and talk to retell the key details. Listen in to assess how much information students are holding on to as they retell:

◆ Do students discuss several pieces of information, rather than rename only the last detail of the information they read?

◆ Do students acquire information from both the illustrations and the text?

◆ Do students keep their talk centered on the information presented in this section of text, or do they stretch back to other parts of the text to retell?

Call students back together after the turn-and-talk, and model a retell a notch or so above the work they're currently doing, with a focus on just this one part of the text. For example, you might say, "If I wanted to retell just this part of the text, listen to how it might go. I could say, 'On this page we learned that it takes years of training to become a knight. We learned that boys start out as a page. They have a master who teaches them all about becoming a knight, and together they practice hunting, fighting, and playing games to improve the boys' abilities.'"

Channel readers to notice how pages go together, putting key details together to determine the main topic of a section.

Next, you might prompt students to think about how the pages go together. You might show how you synthesize the information you just read by touching the pages and saying, "On this page we learned how a boy becomes a page, and on this page we learned about how a page becomes a squire. Then we learned the ways the master helped the squire get ready for knighthood. How do these details go together? What are these pages mostly about?" Model how you look closely at the pages, giving the students time to think alongside you. Then, you might say, "I'm thinking the main topic of this part is becoming a knight. Thumbs up if you were thinking the same thing!"

You may decide to be extra fancy and make an impromptu chapter heading on a Post-it and stick it at the top of page 6 to hold the main topic for your readers.

You might choose to skip pages 4 and 5, the castle chart, because you will refer to the chart during Sessions 1 and 2 in Bend I. Pick up the reading on page 6.

Read on to decide if the next pages go along with the main topic or if they teach about a different main topic.

Prepare students to listen to the next page or two, and ask them to decide if the next pages go along with how to become a knight or if they teach another main topic: "Let's see if the next pages are also about how to become a knight."

Pages 8–9: Pause to gauge students' understanding of the main topics.

After you have read pages 8 and 9, have students turn and talk about what this part teaches. You might say, "Readers, thumbs up if these pages taught more about how to become a knight. Thumbs down if you think this part teaches about something different."

Gauge to see how the readers respond. (You're hoping to see mostly thumbs up. If you see thumbs down, consider voicing over the key details of the pages and modeling how the information fits together under the main topic of becoming a knight.) Confirm the main topic, referring back to the heading you made on page 6, by saying, "You seem to agree that the information on these pages gives more details about becoming a knight. Our heading 'Becoming a Knight' definitely still works! Let's read on."

Pages 10–13: Orchestrate the entire process of restating the key details to determine the main topic.

Before reading on, prepare students for a new main topic by displaying the picture on the document camera and asking, "Now that we know how you become a knight, let's read and think about what this part is teaching us about knights. What do we see? What is happening?"

At the end of page 11, prompt partners to turn and talk to retell the key details learned. Continue to listen in to assess how much information students are holding on to as they retell before rearticulating what you heard in a more sophisticated way.

At page 13, pause to model how you review and accumulate key details from the section. "We just learned a lot of information about knights. We learned that knights had all sorts of weapons—shields and lances and a battle-ax. We also learned that knights wore gear—helmets, chain mail, and armor—to stay safe. Those are some of the details we learned. What's the main topic? If you were going to give these pages a heading, what would you name it? Turn and talk."

Move around from partnership to partnership, coaching in to see if students understand that the pages are mostly about how knights protect themselves. Assess students' understanding as well as their speaking and listening:

◆ Are students naming a main topic using a sentence or a short phrase, or does it sound like one word?

◆ Are students putting the details together to come up with a main topic?

◆ Are students naming more details, moving further away from the main topic?

◆ Are students explaining how they came up with their main topics?

106

Then voice back several student suggestions and add another Post-it to create a new section heading for this chunk of text. For example, you might jot, "How Knights Protect Themselves" and mark the start of the "chapter" on page 10.

Mark the place in the book to pick up reading for the next read-aloud session.

AFTER YOU READ

Review what students have learned so far and ask them to retell the text by naming the main topics and telling key details that go with each part.

As you bring the read-aloud to a close for today, solidify students' learning and help them practice the important skill of retelling by reviewing all that they have learned about knights thus far.

You could prompt students to think about what the book has taught them by saying, "Wow, we've already learned a lot about knights, and we are only halfway through the book. I'll bet your brain is swimming with all sorts of ideas and information. Since there is still more of the book to read, it helps to make sure that you have organized the information you've learned and will be ready to go when you come back to the book. Think of some of the parts you learned about today so that you can retell those parts and act them out so everyone can picture what a knight's life is like."

Quickly rename the main topics alongside the students, "Okay, so what are the big topics this book taught us about? The first part taught us what knights are, and the next part taught us about . . ." Have kids finish the sentence. If students have difficulty, you'll want to turn back to the headings you recorded on Post-its. You might quickly write these on chart paper to help kids organize the information to structure their retell work:

1. What Is a Knight?

2. Becoming a Knight

3. How Knights Protect Themselves

"Okay, we've got the main topics of the first half of *Knights in Shining Armor*. Now let's retell some key details that go with each part. Turn and tell your partner."

Listen to students' key details work, and coach to make sure they are filing the details under the right part and retelling the entire text.

If you hear students focusing in on one main topic to the exclusion of others, you might say, "Wow wowie wow wow! I heard you give some key details about knight protection. You mentioned that knights had weapons for protection and that they wore different gear to protect themselves. Now, choose another part to remember and retell about those

SESSION 1: AFTER YOU READ
p. 13: Review what students have learned so far. Ask them to retell by naming the main topics, telling key details that go with each part, and acting them out.

"It helps to make sure you organize the information you've learned so far. Think about some of the parts you learned about today so you'll be ready to retell those parts and act them out."

knights in shining armor." As you listen to partners talk, prompt students to say a bit more with questions such as "What else did Gail Gibbons teach us?" or "What is an example of that?" or "Why is that important to know?"

It's likely students will retell key details with incorrect main topics as headings. If you hear this, be sure to repeat back what you hear partnerships saying and put it under the right category for readers.

Coach students to act out a page, drawing on information in the illustrations and text to enhance their acting.

Next, you might choose to project a page from the text and coach students as they act out what they are learning. "Another way to learn what a knight's life is like is to become a knight and act out what it's like to be a knight—show how knights moved, how they talked, what they did!" Then, you might project page 6 from the book and say, "Will you and your partner get ready to try this work on this page? Remember, this is all about becoming a knight. Look at the picture while I read the text, and think about what information you'll need to act it out." Then, you might read aloud the page, using your voice to emphasize key details. You might say, "All right, knights, bring this page to life!" Support students in drawing on all the details in the illustrations as well as the text to strengthen their acting.

Support students in growing ideas from the text. Channel students to predict what they expect upcoming parts of the book will teach.

"Now, turn and tell your partner what *you* think about knights. What ideas do you have? What are you starting to think about being a knight? Start like this, 'I think . . . ,' and then remember to add a 'because.' Go!"

After your students share, you might say, "What do we expect the next part of this book will teach us about knights? Any ideas?" You may ask a few students to share their predictions and then say, "We will find out more tomorrow!"

SESSION 2

BEFORE YOU READ

Set readers up to prepare for the second half of the book by recalling what they have learned so far and previewing upcoming sections.

You may decide to start the second read with a quick recap of what children have already learned about knights. You could say, "It's time for us to go back, back, back in time again to the time of knights to learn all about them. So far, we've learned a lot of information about what a knight is, how a boy becomes a knight, and how knights protect themselves." You might decide to flip back in the book to revisit the headings you made for the sections during the first read or display the chart of main topics you created during Session 1. Then, ask children to turn and retell each section.

As you prepare the readers for the second half of the text, you could continue to support the students' practice of close reading by returning to the work of prediction. You might say, "Let's take a sneak peek of the second half of the book. Let's study the illustrations closely and think about what else there is to learn about knights. Then you can turn and talk to your partner about your observations and predictions."

You may decide to slowly flip through pages 15–20 to set the children up to turn and predict with their partners. Listen in and coach as needed. After a minute or two, say back what you hear students predicting.

"Many of you noticed the horses on each page and the different things the knights and horses are doing together. I heard you predict that in the next few pages of the book we might learn about the importance of a knight's horse. Let's get to reading and see if you can confirm your prediction or whether you need to revise your understanding."

AS YOU READ

Prompt students to listen actively, urging them to signal when new main topics are uncovered.

"Let's read the next part to find out what else we can learn about knights. When you think you've figured out what the next section is mostly about—the main topic—put a thumb on your knee." We suggest that you *don't* stop each time a reader's thumb pops up. Instead, when you see a wave of thumbs going up, consider making time for students to turn and talk to share their thinking and understanding.

Pages 14–17: Read aloud a few pages. Set students up to listen and decide how information is changing across the text.

Gauge students' understanding along the way. You could pause to prompt, "What do you think the main topic of this part is? Turn and talk about *how* these pages go together."

You may have to coach readers to notice that the next part has actually shifted to a new main topic by saying, "Now we're learning that knights depended on their horses during battles and also that battles could be small. I'm hearing many of you say that these pages are about something a little different. Now we're learning about knights going into battle." Jot, "Going into Battle" on a Post-it, flipping back to page 14 to place it at the beginning of the section.

Pages 18–21: Ask students to raise questions about what they are learning.

As you read the next couple of pages stop and study each page. You may want to ask students to help you answer questions about the text, such as "What does that mean?" or "What do you see happening?"

Consider prompting students to raise their own questions about the information they are learning. Invite students to turn and talk about the questions they have about battles, and then ask for three or four examples to be shared with the whole group. You might model for students how you can reread the text to see if it can help answer the questions. Then read on. You might say, "As we continue reading, be on the lookout for information that helps answer the questions!"

Pages 22–25: Pause to figure out unfamiliar vocabulary as you read aloud, and channel students to construct definitions using a repertoire of strategies.

You'll want to provide opportunities for students to orchestrate the strategies they will learn to understand unfamiliar keywords. You might pause after reading the second sentence to say, "Captive? What does that mean? This book doesn't have any text features that will help us with this word. What can we do to unlock this word?"

Use the anchor chart from Bend II to review strategies for unlocking an unfamiliar word, and then ask children to turn and work with their partner to figure out what *captive* means and how it adds to their knowledge of knights. After a moment or two, come back together to build a definition. Don't worry if the definition does not perfectly match what a dictionary might say, since the process of pausing to understand new vocabulary is a habit you'll continually prompt readers to rely on.

If you have already taught Session 8 in Bend II, this is an opportunity to apply those strategies in a different context. If you have not taught Session 8, then you will want to model the strategies on the anchor chart.

ANCHOR
CHART

Talk the Talk! Read to Learn the Lingo!

- Expect and look out for keywords.
- Look for and use features to help.
- Use the WHOLE page to figure out what new keywords mean.
- Ask, "What's it like or similar to?

Continue this process with other words as you read on. "There's a word that keeps popping up on the pages of the book. Look, this word, *chivalry*, is on these pages at least three times." Put pages 22 and 23 on the document camera and point out both *chivalry* and *chivalrous*. "It must be something key to understanding knights. I'll reread, and I want you to think about what this means."

Reread pages 22 and 23 and then pause, saying, "Partners, work together to figure out what this word means. Remember to think, 'What does this word teach about knights?'" Then, call students back together and share a definition you heard students construct. Next, you might give students clear language to describe how rereading and using the whole page is helping the class understand the word. "Readers, we reread the part and used the whole page, and this helped us understand that chivalry is good mannered *and* that it was important for a knight to be chivalrous.

Page 28: Pause before reading the page to notice changes in text features and set children up to shift their thinking. Support students in checking their prediction as they read on.

"Hey, we've been adding our own chapter headings to the parts of this book, and look! This part *has* a chapter heading!" Put page 28 under the document camera and show the heading. Set the kids up to think about the importance of the heading by saying, "Turn and tell your partner your best prediction. Why do you think the author used a heading for this part of the text? What are you getting ready to learn about?" Then you might say, "Listen closely as I read to see if your prediction was right or if you learned different information." You might pause at the end of page 28, and say, "Turn and tell your partner. Did your prediction match what the text tells about? Why or why not?"

Pages 29–30: Coach students to think of a heading for the final section of the book.

You might decide to mask the section heading, "Dragon Legends," before saying, "Guess what? *This* section has a heading, too. A different heading. I've covered it up to see if you can figure out what this part is mostly about. I'll read the information, and you think about what this page is mostly about. Listen and think about what you would name these pages."

Read to the end of the book and then have students turn and talk to come up with possible headings. "Turn and tell your partner what these pages were mostly about and what you would name this section." After a bit, call students back together and listen as they offer suggestions for the heading title.

Guide students to check their prediction against the actual heading and to consider why the author chose a particular heading for that section.

Jot the student suggestions onto chart paper, and then reveal the actual heading. "Hmm, . . . Gail Gibbons titled this section 'Dragon Legends.' How does that match up with what you predicted? Why do you think the author chose that heading? What does she want you to understand about these knights?"

AFTER YOU READ

Set students up for a whole-class conversation. Give partnerships a few minutes to talk together to prepare before discussing with the class.

Have students quickly form a circle in the meeting area so the conversation can begin. When students are settled, say, "We learned a lot of information about knights from Gail's book. Turn and tell your partner some of the important information you learned about knights in shining armor."

Move around the circle and listen in to student conversations. Jot student responses onto oversized Post-it notes or chart paper, making sure you have a couple of ideas to lead the upcoming whole-class conversation, if needed to keep the conversation going.

Remind students of expectations for growing ideas during whole-class conversations. Draw their attention to charts and earlier experiences.

After a couple of minutes, call the students back together and begin the conversation. You might remind children of how to talk long and strong about a book. "Remember, to talk long and strong about our ideas, you can share your thinking

---

SESSION 2: AFTER YOU READ

End: Set students up for a whole-class conversation.

"We learned a lot of information about _____. Turn and tell your partner some of the important information you learned. Remember, you can share your thinking or ask the class a question by saying, 'I wonder _____?' Use our 'Readers TALK About Books' chart to help you."

or ask a question out to the class by saying, 'I wonder . . .' You can also get the conversation started by talking about things you learned. Use our 'Readers TALK About Books' chart to help you."

Readers TALK About Books

"I think . . . because . . ."

"I wonder . . . maybe . . ."

"I can add on . . ."

"Why do you think that?"

"Can you show that in the book?"

While you may not need to remind students of conversation protocol, you might tuck in a quick reminder: "Remember to use your best manners to talk. Eyes on the speaker. One voice at a time. Hands down and minds on. Listen carefully so you can *add* on and keep the talk going. Who'd like to start our talk today?"

Engage the class in conversation, recalling and thinking about parts of and responses to the text. Coach students to grow text-based ideas and ensure that all students participate.

Turn your voice off and look out into the audience, signaling that conversation should begin. If children begin the conversation naturally, let them continue the conversation as you listen in and assess talk. As you listen in, make sure that talk is growing across students and that they are adding on to one another's conversation. You might need to redirect the class or use the prompt "Let's get back to the book," if you notice talk veering far away from the text. Then, too, you might transfer this responsibility to students and let them be the decision makers when they think talk is getting off topic.

If, and only if, there is a lull in the conversation or students get way off topic, rejoin the conversation to get the talk back on track by using one of the comments you collected and jotted on a Post-it note at the start of the conversation. Weaving in a turn-and-talk at these points gives students time to orient themselves to the new topic of conversation and allows them to rehearse some ideas with a partner before sharing with the class. This often supports a surge in ideas. As students turn and talk, you might move to a new part of the circle and sit behind a student who could get the class back on track. Whisper in to encourage a student to relaunch the conversation when you call the class back together.

Remember that there are multiple ways for students to participate in the conversation. You might move to quiet parts of the conversation as you listen in and encourage those not taking part in the conversation to add their thinking or to show understanding by nodding and eye contact. You might also intersperse partner talk throughout the whole-class conversation to ensure that all students are discussing ideas, even if they are not sharing with the whole class.

Assess students' abilities to determine author's purpose through an individual stop-and-jot.

"Readers, it's clear that this book has you interested in the topic of knights. You thought about the important information Gail Gibbons taught about knights. You talked about your thinking about knights and their way of life. You weren't just naming out facts from the book; you shared your thinking and questions about the topic. Before you head back to your seats, take a moment to think about the author, Gail Gibbons. Think about this: What do you think Gail Gibbons wants you to know or understand about knights? What does she want to teach about knights? Why, do you think, did she write the book? Stop and jot your idea on your Post-it note." Collect the Post-it notes to gauge students understanding.

◆ Are students naming the topic of the book (knights), or are they naming what the author wants them to think about knights?

◆ Are students naming what the author wants them to think on one page, or do their thoughts encompass the whole book?

◆ Are students naming ideas that are supported by details in the text?

Set a purpose for rereading the text, and ask students to consider parts that helped them understand the author's purpose.

Have students turn one last time to talk about their thinking. Listen in to determine students' specific thinking around author's purpose. For example, you might look for children who thought the author's purpose was to have the reader understand how knights were brave and skilled warriors. You might highlight this for the class, saying, "A lot of you think Gail wrote this book to teach us that knights were brave and skilled! Next time we read this book, we can reread and compare parts that help us understand how brave and skilled knights were. What parts might help us understand this better? Which parts should we reread? Turn and tell your partners which three parts you think we should study next time." Mark the parts students suggest with a Post-it note so they are easy to refer back to.

SESSION 3

BEFORE YOU READ

Review students' ideas about the author's purpose.

We suggest that today you reread to compare selected parts of the book that will engage students in thinking more deeply about the author's purpose, or why the author wrote the book. Before you read, remind students of the work they did during the previous read-aloud session when they considered the author's purpose and chose the parts of the texts they will reread to compare and accumulate information that supports that purpose. You might say, "Last time we read *Knights in Shining Armor*, we thought about how Gail wanted to teach us how knights were brave and skilled

All authors have a purpose for writing what they do. Sometimes they have more than one! Gail Gibbons clearly has lots of information to share with her readers; she wrote to inform. But her information may also be interesting or even entertaining to some readers, so one could say that her writing both informs and entertains or engages. Your instruction here will get students thinking about why an author writes (a concept that is important when students do their own writing), but it is not necessary to use the term author's purpose at this point.

warriors, and we marked some of pages we thought we could study that would help us understand this better—pages about how boys became knights, how knights protect themselves, and how they prepare to go into battle."

AS YOU READ

Recruit students to think more deeply about the text as you reread sections of it. Alternate between reading, partner talk, and sharing students' ideas with the class.

As you reread to compare various parts of the book, remind students to angle the way they listen to the text, keeping the author's purpose in mind as they think more deeply about the information. Perhaps you'll say, "As we read about knights, let's think about how Gail Gibbons uses the pictures and words to help us understand just how knights were brave and skilled warriors."

Then reread the selected parts, pausing to have readers turn and talk about what they are thinking along the way. For example, after rereading the part about how a boy becomes a knight on pages 7–9, you might say, "How does this information help us understand that knights were either brave and/or skilled warriors?"

Then after a few minutes you might rearticulate some of their responses, saying, "Some of you said that this part helps you understand that knights are skilled because they go through years of training before being granted knighthood. They have a master that helps them learn to play games to build their skills, and they even get to ride by his side in battle. Some of you said that this part helps you understand that knights are brave because they start training as young as seven years old! I heard some of you say that's how old you are! Can you imagine what it would be like to be training to be a knight?"

Reestablish a focus before reading on. You might say, "Gail Gibbons is totally helping us to see how knights were some of the most skilled and brave warriors in history! We reread to understand how intricate their training was. Let's keep reading to find even more information!"

Continue to revisit and compare other parts of the text to confirm the author's purpose. You might reread the part about how knights protect themselves on pages 10–15, as well as the part about battles on pages 18–21. Consider pausing after a couple of pages to monitor for understanding. For example, at the end of page 11, you might say, "So, how does the information in this part help us understand just how brave and skilled knights were? Look closely at this picture. What do you notice? How does that fit with what the words say?"

Give students a few more opportunities to turn and talk, encouraging them to name examples from the text that help them to support the author's purpose.

AFTER YOU READ

Invite students to engage in conversations centered around the author's purpose.

At the end of rereading and talking about various sections of the text, you might give your students an opportunity to talk about the author's purpose in small groups in the meeting area. You might say, "Let's discuss in our groups information Gail Gibbons taught us to help us understand how knights were brave and skilled warriors." You might project a page of the text as groups talk to deepen conversation.

After brief conversations in small groups, you might bring students back together for a quick symphony share. Ask your students to sit in a large circle. Then ask them to share the information that supported the author's purpose. You may say to your students, "So, as I point to you and wave my baton, say what you think helps readers know how brave and skilled knights were. Here we go! Get ready to share!" And I picked up my pretend baton and pointed to the first student.

SESSION 3: AFTER YOU READ

End: Invite students to engage in conversations centered around the author's purpose.

"In our groups, let's discuss information the author taught us to help us understand that _____. As I point to you and wave my baton, name the important details that support the author's purpose. Here we go! Get ready to share!"

Shared Reading
Becoming Experts

Text Selection

> *Tigers*, by Laura Marsh

> Song or poem of your choice—preferably about tigers or animals, for example, "I Just Can't Wait to Be King" from *The Lion King*

Since books at these levels are often too long to read in one sitting, we suggest focusing just on a few chapters. We've selected a few from *Tigers*, by Laura Marsh, to read and reread across the week. This text is part of the *National Geographic Kids* series and is chock full of engaging information, gorgeous photographs, and helpful text features. The chapters we selected are "A Tiger's Home" (starting on page 6), "Cubs" (starting on page 16), and "Tigers in Trouble" (starting on page 24), and they lend themselves perfectly to practicing the skills that nonfiction readers use when reading to grow knowledge. The passages should be enlarged on a document camera. They were strategically selected to be different from the passages referenced in Bend II. The passages will, however, be revisited again in Bend III as the demonstration text to hold against the other text about tigers when readers are asked to grow knowledge by reading across books.

DAY ONE: Warm Up, Book Introduction, and First Read

On the first day, it will be important to introduce the book in a way that gets kids excited to revisit it again and again across the week. From the very start, you'll invite children to think and read alongside you, explaining that together you'll read selections from the text together, practicing the many things that all readers—especially nonfiction readers—do.

In this unit, readers are encouraged to grow knowledge—noticing details and putting them together, asking questions, and accumulating new learning. This, too, will be the goal as you approach this shared reading text—orchestrating the active meaning making that is necessary when reading to gain information. It will also be important to reactivate and support the transference of the skills and strategies that were strengthened during Unit 1, as well as in first grade.

WARM UP: "I Just Can't Wait to Be King"

Quickly introduce and read a poem or song related to the content area to build genre awareness, fluency, and excitement.

Read a poem or song that provides some information about a topic children are reading about. You might choose something to do with tigers or animals to demonstrate that you can read about a topic in a variety of genres.

Children love reading and singing lyrics from favorite songs such as those in *The Lion King* or *The Jungle Book*. You might choose the favorite "I Just Can't Wait to Be King" and say, "Readers, it's not only in nonfiction books that we hear about the topics we've been growing knowledge about! There are songs and poems about them too! You might know this one from *The Lion King*. Let's sing 'I Just Can't Wait to Be King' together! What's fun about this song is that it's got two characters in it—Simba and Zazu—and they each sing different parts. I wrote Simba's parts in red and Zazu's parts in blue so we can tell the difference. Today, let's all sing both parts! Get your best singing voices ready!"

You might read only part of the song today, stopping midway through the song to say, "Wow! You sounded gorgeous! I love how you tried to scoop up the words in each line as you sang it! I love how you made certain words pop! Isn't it cool there are songs and poems about animals, too? This poem isn't about tigers, but it's about another big cat—lions!

"Let's reread one more time. As we read, think, 'What does this song teach us about lions?'

"Okay, with your partner, will you turn and talk about what this part of the song taught us about the big cats, lions? Go!" You will then want to spend a short time retelling what this part of the song was mostly about before getting ready to read a new book together.

DAY ONE FOCUS

✔ Getting to know the shared reading book

✔ Taking a sneak peek to anticipate information

✔ Applying word-solving skills from Unit 1

GETTING READY

✔ Prepare a copy of a song or poem about tigers or other animals to sing with students. We suggest "I Just Can't Wait to Be King" from *The Lion King*. Make sure the copy is large enough for all students to read, or be ready to project it (see Warm Up).

✔ Prepare to share chapters from a familiar text a level or two above the reading level of most of your students. Here we suggest "A Tiger's Home," "Cubs," and "Tigers in Trouble" from *Tigers*, by Laura Marsh (see Book Introduction and First Reading).

✔ Cover three to five words or parts of words in the chapters you select (See Book Introduction and First Reading).

✔ Display the anchor chart "Nonfiction Readers Grow Knowledge" (see After Reading).

BOOK INTRODUCTION AND FIRST READING: *Tigers*, by Laura Marsh

Give a book introduction that gets readers excited to learn. Invite children to anticipate information by taking a sneak peek.

Begin by talking about why you chose the book, and then preview the text together, anticipating the information that you would expect in each part. If you have already introduced *Tigers*, by Laura Marsh, in Session 4, then use this time to remind children of that work, perhaps lessening the scaffolds and allowing them to take the lead on where to look to figure out how the book goes.

You might say, "Readers, I'm beyond giddy to share this book that we can grow knowledge from. We are so lucky to have so many fabulous books to choose from! This one is called *Tigers*, and it is filled with information that we can read to become tiger experts! Some of you might already know some information about tigers. That rocks!" Holding the book under the document camera, point to the title page and add, "But Laura Marsh wrote this book for readers like you, so you need to give her your undivided attention right from the start! Laura is *such* a wonderful teacher. She thought about everything she knew about tigers and made this book to teach it to us, part by part, across these beautiful pages."

Flip through a few pages, gushing over the photographs and words, before suggesting, "Why don't we take a sneak peek? Let's preview *all* of the different parts of the book to get ready for the information we might learn!"

Stop to ponder some possibilities together by asking, "What might we learn about tigers in this book? Turn and tell your partner!" Listen in to some partnerships and listen for their predictions before naming some options. Try to rearticulate the detail within the larger context of the topic. For example, you might say, "Stella said that we might learn that tigers live in the jungle! We might learn about where tigers live. Thumbs up if you agree! Esteban said that we might learn that tigers eat deer! Do you think we will learn about what tigers eat? Put up a thumb if you think so!"

Use features to revise and focus information predictions.

"Let's preview the different parts that we will read together to anticipate what information we might learn in *each* part!" Open the book to the table of contents and move your finger down the page, pausing especially at the chapters that have been selected.

Stop on, "A Tiger's Home" and ask, "This chapter is called 'A Tiger's Home.' What might we learn about tigers in this part?" Turn to page 6 and let partnerships turn and predict before saying, "Yes, I agree! In this chapter, we'll probably learn about where tigers live!"

Then flip back to the table of contents and tap the chapter titled "Cubs." Open to page 16 and stop briefly before turning to page 18, where the chapter continues. "What about in this part?" Repeat this process for "Tigers in Trouble."

A Tiger's Home

Tigers live in the forest. They spend a lot of time in the water, too. They live in hot places like Indonesia. They live in cold places like Russia.

Indochinese Tiger

6

Invite children to read the selected passages alongside you, with lots of expression and fluency right from the start.

Read through the selected passages with lots of expression and fluency. (In information books, you'll lead students to sound like an expert by reading with an authoritative narrator or documentarian voice.) To get more kids to chime in on the first read, you might say things like "I hear some great reporting voices," or "Can you help me read that part again and make it sound more interesting and lively?"

Select three to five words or parts of words to cover. Stop to practice using multiple sources of information to figure out and check the word.

You will also want to prepare a few places to practice word solving on a first read. Select three to five different words or parts of words to cover so that students can practice word solving and orchestrating meaning, syntax (or structure), and visual information (MSV) to solve unknown words. When covering a whole word, prompt readers to use meaning first, making a few guesses of what would make sense by using the context of the book and prior knowledge. Do not praise accuracy; rather, praise persistence and flexibility, complimenting students who are able to come up with multiple possibilities that make sense and sound right. Then uncover parts of the word to check for visual information, slowly revealing the whole word before confirming. Then, reread to smooth out the sentence.

Other times, you might choose to cover part of a word. For example on page 8, you might cover the ending of the word *forest*. "'Tigers live in the for–' What would make sense here?" Children will likely guess the word. You could then prompt, "Forest? Would that make sense? Does that sound right?" Then, cross-check visual information, "If the word is forest, what would the next part of the word look like? Jot it in the air with your finger! Now, let's reveal!" Peeling the Post-it off of the word, children will cheer, "-*est*! It's *forest*!" Again, reread the sentence in a smooth voice before reading on and pausing at other covered words or word parts.

AFTER READING

Set students up to reread all (or one part) together to accumulate new learning.

After reading through the chapters, you might go back and reread the chapter "A Tiger's Home," helping children accumulate information, holding on to more key details from the text. You might refer to the "Nonfiction Readers Grow Knowledge" anchor chart to reinforce the strategies children have learned thus far and are practicing independently during reading workshop.

Nonfiction Readers Grow Knowledge

- Pay attention to details.
- Put the parts of the text together in your mind.
- Ask questions.
- Think, "What is this book (and this part) teaching me?"

It will be important to remind children to pay attention to all the details in the text, putting them together to determine the main topic of each section. You might say, "Readers, you just grew some knowledge about tigers. Remember that you need to notice *all* the details on the page and put the information together to think, 'What is this part teaching me?' Then, you can give examples about each to retell what you've learned."

Use features to determine importance.

Before rereading, demonstrate how headings serve as helpful containers to organize details that go together. You might say, "We used this heading, 'A Tiger's Home,' to predict what this chapter would teach us. *Now*, we can use this heading to help us retell what we learned about where tigers live. Let's reread and keep track of what we learned about where tigers live."

Consider pausing to notice how the photographs and other graphics confirm or add to information in the text. Point back and forth asking, "How do the pictures and words go together? Does the picture teach us anything that the words don't?" You might use other features, such as captions, to add more learning. Reread the captions on pages 6 and 7 together and prompt, "What does this caption teach us about tigers?" Additionally, you might choose to add a label or a caption on photographs that don't include these features, as a way to help students to voice back learning.

Coach partners to retell the information.

After rereading, help children synthesize the information, possibly revising (or adding) a heading to name the main topic of the section. You might ask, "What else might we call this section?" For example, after reading "A Tiger's Home," you might decide that "Where Tigers Live" or "Tigers Live in Many Places" would be alternative names for the part. Then, coach partners to use the heading to teach back important information learned across the pages.

On this day, you'll reread both the familiar poem or song you've chosen and the specific sections of *Tigers*, focusing on cross-checking words using all three sources of information. You'll spend time prompting and looking at words to help students think about *how* they can confirm their reading to monitor accuracy. Help them use MSV to check in with their reading, both when they read accurately and when they miscue. Students need to understand that after checking their attempt they either need to make another attempt and try again or verify that their attempt is correct and keep on reading. If you only ever model checking when you've made an error, students may not realize that they also need to check even when they've gotten it right.

WARM UP: "I Just Can't Wait to Be King"

Reread yesterday's song, revealing the remaining verses. Readers at levels J/K/L require knowledge of how to take longer words apart in various ways. You'll want to decide on which words you'll use to practice this work, using highlighter tape to draw extra attention to these words across the read. You might highlight *enemies* and *uninspiring*, among others. As you read through the song, stop on these words to prompt students to check for meaning and syntax. Then slide your finger under the word as children check through all the parts, confirming that it looks right. Be sure to reread each line in a smooth and fluent voice.

SECOND READING: "Cubs" from *Tigers*, by Laura Marsh

Remind readers to continue using all they know to solve words and to check that they are reading with accuracy.

Today you'll focus on the chapter "Cubs," which begins on page 16. You'll want to be ready to compliment and prompt the work children do as they stop to tackle tricky words. You might drop your voice as children read aloud, listening for words readers do not recognize with automaticity. Prompt readers by saying, "You might know this word, but you might not! What can we do to figure this out?" To keep language consistent to develop the inner ear of a proficient reader, nudge partnerships to look at the chart you developed during Unit 1, and apply these known strategies to figure out tricky words:

DAY TWO FOCUS

✔ Orchestrating information by asking, "Does it make sense, sound right, and look right?" to check words (cross-checking)

✔ Rereading for comprehension

✔ Developing more fluency

GETTING READY

✔ Display a copy of the song or poem you used yesterday (see Warm Up).

✔ Prepare to share a chapter from the familiar text you read yesterday with students. Here we reread "Cubs" from *Tigers* (see Second Reading).

✔ Display the anchor chart "When Words Are Tricky, Roll Up Your Sleeves!" from Unit 1 (see Second Reading).

> ### When Words Are Tricky, Roll Up Your Sleeves!
>
> - Check the picture, and think, "What would make sense?"
> - Use what's happening in the story.
> - Look through the WHOLE word, part-by-part.
> - Look for a word inside a word.
> - Don't give up! Try something! Take a guess!

You might stop on the word *weigh* and say, "This is a tricky one! Let's roll up our sleeves! What can we do? 'The cubs _____ about four pounds at birth.' What are we learning about here?" Give kids a moment to mull over the possibilities before moving forward, "Some of you think it says, 'weigh.'" As you move through the strategies, prompt the students to stop occasionally, using the three cueing systems to cross-check. "Wait, did that word make sense, sound right, and look right?" you'll say. "Let's check it!" Readers at levels J/K/L will especially need opportunities to practice solving multisyllabic words. You might pause on words that readers will have to break into more parts to be sure it looks right, such as *otherwise*, *together*, *usually,* and *territories*.

At times you'll check even when the words are correct. For example, you might read, "The cubs weigh about four pounds at birth." Stopping on *pounds*, you could say, "How do we know that is the word *pounds*? Does that make sense? Does that sound right? Does that look right? Let's be absolutely sure!" At other times you may intentionally read a word incorrectly and have students check as well. For example, at the bottom of page 16 you might cover all but the *a* in the word *alone*. You might say, "'Otherwise, adult tigers live apart.' That makes sense. Let's look through the *whole* word, part by part, to be sure." Revealing the rest of the word you might say, "*Apart* ends with /t/ but there's no *t*. This can't be *apart*! What would make sense, sound right, *and* look right?"

You'll want to help children develop the habit that whenever they are unsure, they check; sometimes they'll be right and sometimes they won't. You might say, "Readers, since this is a tricky word, let's check it!" Always follow this up with, "Were we right? How do you know?" It is useful to have children name the strategies they use to solve words. "Point to the part of the chart that helped you," you might say. By having kids think about what strategies they are using, you are extending their independence and metacognition.

AFTER READING

Practice synthesizing and retelling information.

It will be important to keep comprehension of the text alive! Continue to practice the retelling work you began on the first day, except now release some of the scaffolds so that the children are constructing more than they did the prior day. Let kids lean on you as you use the whole page—headings, pictures, labels, and captions—to remind them how to think about how the parts go together to teach important information about tigers.

Coach kids to be curious by asking and answering questions.

It's important that children understand that nonfiction readers grow knowledge by thinking and raising questions about what they are reading. Talk about how as readers of nonfiction they are learning a lot of new information and, therefore, it's important for them to observe closely and develop ideas and questions as they read. "We just grew a lot of knowledge about tigers by studying this section about tiger cubs. What questions do you have? What are you wondering?" You might even have students stop and jot their questions to then share with partners. Encourage partnerships to attempt to answer their questions, before collecting them to revisit after tomorrow's session.

DAY THREE: Word Study

On this third read of the text, you'll focus on the phonics work level J/K/L readers need to solidify when word solving, as well as developing more fluency and comprehension. You'll also focus on vocabulary, bringing attention to the keywords authors use to teach about a topic. Ensure that readers are monitoring and learning as much information as they can from their books by stopping to figure out and use keywords. You'll demonstrate how students will be able to define some words easily because they are defined explicitly in a text feature, while other words will take more work to define.

WARM UP: "I Just Can't Wait to Be King"

Revisit the same song, each time building automaticity, fluency, and comprehension. You'll want to compliment students' efforts to reread and practice, supporting both confidence and engagement. Since today focuses on vocabulary, consider focusing on some words children might be unfamiliar with or that are key to understanding the content. Stop at vocabulary words to build definitions together. Prompt readers to consider how the word teaches even more about the topic. Then reread the line in a voice that reflects an understanding of the words within it.

DAY THREE FOCUS

- ✔ Exploring word study patterns and concepts
- ✔ Studying vocabulary and word choice to deepen comprehension

GETTING READY

- ✔ Display a copy of the song or poem you used yesterday (see Warm Up).
- ✔ Prepare to share chapters from the familiar text you read yesterday with students. Here we reread "Cubs" and "Tigers in Trouble" from *Tigers* (see Third Reading).
- ✔ Display the anchor chart "Talk the Talk! Read to Learn the Lingo!" (see Third Reading).
- ✔ Make sure children have access to their book baggies (see After Reading).
- ✔ Provide index cards or Post-its for children to collect words on (see After Reading).
- ✔ Hang a pocket chart in which you will collect children's words (see After Reading).

THIRD READING: "Cubs" from *Tigers*, by Laura Marsh

Use the text as a means to focus on the phonics work that readers at this band of text complexity need.

You'll want to pick a word study focus for this day, focusing especially on the phonics work that level J/K/L readers need. Consider focusing on long vowel patterns, multisyllabic words, compound words, and/or plurals. Reread "Cubs," mining the passage in search of specific spelling patterns. For example, if focusing on long vowel patterns, point out the vowel combination *ai* in *raises* or *eigh* in *weigh*. You might also support students' flexibility with words by pointing out the different sounds vowels can make, such as *r*-controlled vowels (for example, *ir* in *birth*) or diphthongs (for example, *ou* in *pounce*).

Your assessment data might also show that many of your students need work with high-frequency words. There are several in the passages that you might choose to highlight, such as *about*, *together*, *come*, *their*, *only*, *have*, *they*, and *when*. Highlight a few and say, "When we get to these words, I want you to stop and try to picture the whole word in your head. Then, let's reread them in a snap!"

Study unfamiliar vocabulary, using text features to determine meaning.

As you read "Cubs," demonstrate how text features can help readers understand keywords. It's important to focus this work on *using* these features to help deepen understanding of the topic, not merely naming the feature. Guide children to look closely at the photos, diagrams, and other features to consider how the text works with these features to help them understand the keywords.

For example, when you get to the word *territories* on page 21, you can say, "Might a feature help us with this keyword?" Search the pages of the chapter before flipping to the glossary to discover the defined word. After reading to learn the definition, remind children to go back to the sentence, to reread and ask, "What does this word teach you about tigers? We're learning that when tigers are two they leave their family to find their own area to protect!" Next, move to the chapter "Tigers in Trouble," practicing a similar process of using features to understand keywords (such as *endangered*, *extinct*, and *habitat*, which are defined in special text boxes on pages 24–26) to grow knowledge of a topic.

Support readers in understanding words that are not defined in features, using the whole page to build definitions together.

The domain-specific words that are defined in a text are not the only ones that might be unfamiliar to students yet necessary to help readers learn more about the topic. You might pause at *raises*, *otherwise*, *pounce*, and *traditional*, saying, "Readers, not *all* words are defined in features, but don't worry. There are many ways to figure out what keywords mean." Use the anchor chart "Talk the Talk! Read to Learn the Lingo!" to focus on strategies that can help readers figure out what keywords mean:

Talk the Talk! Read to Learn the Lingo!

- Expect and look out for keywords.
- Look for and use features to help.
- Use the WHOLE page to figure out what new keywords mean.
- Ask, "What's it like or similar to?"

In addition, you might prompt, "Maybe this means . . . ," "It could be . . . ," "This is like . . . ," "There is a clue in the picture that makes me think . . . ," or "What kind of word is this?" After determining the kind of word, if it's a verb, you might say, "Let's all stop and act it out." Or if it's a noun or adjective, add a Post-it to the page to label the word in a picture and/or sketch the word.

Study author's craft, particularly word choice, to deepen students' understanding of the text.

Word choice might be another angle to consider on this day. You might nudge children to think, "Why might the author have chosen *this* word?" Remind kids of the words authors use to describe actions or descriptions in precise ways. Direct their attention to page 19, saying, "What if the author had said, 'Tiger cubs play games'? But, instead, Laura wrote, 'They chase, leap, and pounce.' These words teach us so much more! They describe the action so we can see it!"

AFTER READING

Support transference of word study by facilitating word hunts.

Invite kids to search their book baggies for the word patterns that match the focus you selected for today. You might have them collect these words on index cards to sort, do some interactive writing, or put in their writing folder as a spelling tool. Children might also hunt for the words authors have chosen to use when explaining the topic. You'll ask, "What words do informational writers use to make their teaching really precise? How do they pick words to describe the way something moves or even the way something looks?" Collect the words on Post-its or index cards and put them in a pocket chart to use as a revision tool during writing workshop.

Retell parts of the text, incorporating keywords to demonstrate a larger understanding of the information.

After today's reading, discuss the lingo learned and use these keywords to talk the tiger talk. Have readers revise the retells they gave on prior days, this time incorporating as many keywords as possible when they do it. You might try this together with either "A Tiger's Home" or "Cubs" before encouraging partnerships to do the same with "Tigers in Trouble." It might be helpful to jot the keywords that go with each part and encourage partners to notice and keep track of how often they say the keywords to talk and teach about tigers.

To close this session, remind readers of the importance of always being curious. Revisit questions from the second day and check in to see if any have been answered, before pausing to consider new questions.

DAY FOUR: Fluency

This read will focus on helping readers to become increasingly fluent. You'll aim to focus on developing readers' pace, parsing, and prosody. Prosody involves making sure the text sounds like natural speech. You will help your children listen to their reading to check that it makes sense and sounds right to support phrasing, intonation, and stress.

WARM UP: "I Just Can't Wait to Be King"

Reread the song again, explaining how accuracy, fluency, and comprehension improve with each read. On this reread, you'll want to prompt readers to scoop up more words, noticing how line breaks and/or punctuation help guide the reader. Encourage readers to match their reading voices to the way the text wants to be read: in other words, to convey the overall tone and feeling of the text. You might divide the song into parts across partnerships so that Partner 1 and Partner 2 are reading different lines, reciting the song in two voices. Invite kids to choreograph some movements and use facial expressions to bring the song to life.

FOURTH READING: "Tigers in Trouble" from *Tigers*, by Laura Marsh

Reread the book to work on reading smoothly with both fluency and meaning.

Provide the opportunity to reread like an expert. Help children practice reading with better stress, phrasing, and intonation, with a particular angle on making the reading sound informative. You might use the chapter "Tigers in Trouble." Remind readers that when stopping to tackle tricky words and/or figure out keywords, their reading can start to sound rough and choppy. You'll explain the importance of rereading these parts so that they can be read smoothly and show students' understanding. For example, on pages 24–27, words such as *endangered*, *extinct*, and *habitat* are defined in text boxes. Other words, such as *Bengal* and *Indochinese*, are supported through a pronunciation helper. After stopping to monitor for meaning say, "After you stop to figure out a tricky word, be sure to go back and reread to make your reading sound smooth and to show you understand!" Emphasize that because these words are important to understanding the topic, students will need to read them slowly, or with greater emphasis, to get their meaning across.

DAY FOUR FOCUS

✔ Reading with fluency (appropriate pacing, parsing, and prosody)

✔ Reading for meaning

GETTING READY

✔ Display a copy of the song or poem you used yesterday (see Warm Up).

✔ Prepare to share a chapter from the familiar text you read yesterday with students. Here we reread "Tigers in Trouble" from *Tigers* (see Fourth Reading).

✔ Prepare to share a second chapter from the familiar text you read yesterday with students. Here we reread "Cubs" from *Tigers* (see After Reading).

Tigers in Trouble

Siberian Tiger

Asia

South China Tiger

Bengal Tiger

Indochinese Tiger

Pacific Ocean

Indian Ocean

Sumatran Tiger

Where tigers used to live
Where tigers live today

Tigers are endangered. About 100 years ago, there were 100,000 tigers in the wild. Today there are less than 3,500.

24

There are five different kinds of tigers today. They are the Bengal (BEN-gol), South China, Indochinese (in-doh-chi-NEEZ), Sumatran (soo-MAH-truhn), and Siberian (si-BEER-ee-uhn) tiger. Three other kinds of tigers have already become extinct.

Tiger Term
ENDANGERED: At risk of dying out
EXTINCT: A group of animals no longer living

25

Move on to other sentences and ask students to think about which words they should emphasize, or "give power to," while reading. Have students experiment with a couple of sentences by placing the emphasis on different words. Discuss why some ways sound better than others, or fit better with the meaning of the text.

Coach readers to attend to punctuation as a way to support students' ability to parse the text into meaningful chunks.

You'll want readers to think about their phrasing, taking bigger scoops and using punctuation to gauge how much information to include. They may practice rereading parts with various types of phrasing to figure out which sounds better. On page 24, you might point out how commas help guide the reader. Read, "About 100 years ago," in one scoop before pausing and reading in another scoop, "there were 100,000 tigers in the wild." Transfer this idea to pages 25 and 26, where commas continue to support phrasing.

Have kids do some interpretation work and think about the tone that they should use when reading.

To support intonation, ask readers to think about their reactions to the text. Then have them reread a part to make their voices match the feeling. For example, you might ask readers to think about the part that says, "Today there are less than 3,500 [tigers]." They'll want to think about how that information makes them feel and consider their reactions to that information. "That's *a lot* less than 100 years ago when there were 100,000! This is shocking! It's also very worrisome. Let's reread it together to show this tone in our voices!"

AFTER READING

Reread another chapter to practice rereading like experts to bring the information to life.

Revisit "Cubs" to give children practice with rereading like an expert. Remind readers to think about the number of scoops they read with each breath, noticing and using punctuation to guide them. In some sentences, you might cover punctuation and have children use the meaning of the sentence to predict what type of punctuation would make sense and sound right.

Remind readers to read with expression, prompting them to think about the feeling of the information and to read in a voice that matches the content. After rereading the chapter you might even have children act out parts to bring the information to life. Page 19 lends itself to this nicely. You could say, "Partner 1, you'll get to be the cubs first! Partner 2, you're going to read in a way that lets your partner know what to do!"

Celebrate the work students have done reading and rereading the text, allowing the class to lead this final read, orchestrating all they have learned across the week. Then, consider ways you might extend the text, leading the class in a whole-group discussion, sharing questions or responses to the text, or perhaps even engaging in shared writing to compose a review—or even a persuasive letter or petition.

WARM UP: "I Just Can't Wait to Be King"

Prompt students to recite the words of the song or poem with little to no teacher support.

Reread the song or poem, finding innovative ways to divide it up with different voices or reading different parts. Whichever way you read it, make sure you have a lot of participation and energy.

FINAL READING: *Tigers*, by Laura Marsh

Emphasize how using all three sources of information (MSV) while reading, along with rereading, can make your reading so much stronger.

During your final read of this text, let your students know that they will now practice everything they have tried this week. Revisiting all three passages, they'll read tricky words and use what they know about vocabulary, vowel patterns, and punctuation to read like an expert with great expression and fluency. Allow students' voices to outshine your own, perhaps even letting your voice drop out entirely, instead offering lean prompts that support readers through the passages.

AFTER READING

Facilitate a book talk to celebrate the fun everyone has had reading these chapters over and over again.

Revisit each of the three chapters, inviting readers not just to retell each chapter but to retell the topic. Support readers by saying, "In the first chapter we learned about . . . , in the next chapter we learned about . . . , and yesterday, in the part called "Tigers in Trouble," we learned about . . ."

You might engage students in smaller discussions. Break your students up into three smaller groups, each engaging in a book talk about one chapter. Give students a couple of copies of the text. Ask students to act and talk like experts about one chapter. Say to your students, "Let's try to talk long and strong about the chapter. Use all that you know to help you talk back and listen to one another."

DAY FIVE FOCUS

✔ Reading to orchestrate and use everything students have learned this week

GETTING READY

✔ Display a copy of the song or poem you used yesterday (see Warm Up).

✔ Prepare to share the chapters you have read with students during shared reading (see Final Reading).

✔ Copy the chapters you have read to distribute to students (see After Reading).

You might instead have a whole-class book talk focusing on speaking and listening skills. You might ask children to come up with big ideas or questions they still have about the topic. Or you could focus their conversation on determining importance by considering what the author really wants us to know about the topic. As students share their thoughts and ideas, be sure to return to those parts and put them up on the document camera. Have the student(s) reread parts to support their statements and questions.

Compose a class piece to extend the text, perhaps using shared writing to create a petition in response to the information gleaned from the shared reading.

You may do some shared writing in response to the text, particularly if the information sparked strong reactions and feelings. You might say, "Not only did we learn where tigers live and facts about tiger cubs, but we also learned that tigers are endangered! That made many of us feel shocked and even worried. Maybe we can help! Let's work together to write a petition to help save the tigers. Then, we can invite people in the school to sign it and work together to help make a change!" Invite children to work together to compose the petition, thinking about what important information from the text to include to persuade people to sign it. You might find a time to collect signatures, perhaps posting it in the hallway outside your classroom. Who knows; you may even inspire children to become activists for worthy causes!

Replicate the work of this shared reading plan across other parts of the same text and new texts altogether.

In the coming weeks, you may decide to read the other chapters in *Tigers* during shared reading. You also may decide to read other texts about big cats or to choose a different topic altogether. This way, students who are reading about things other than animals learn ways to talk and think about those types of books as well.